John Cohen

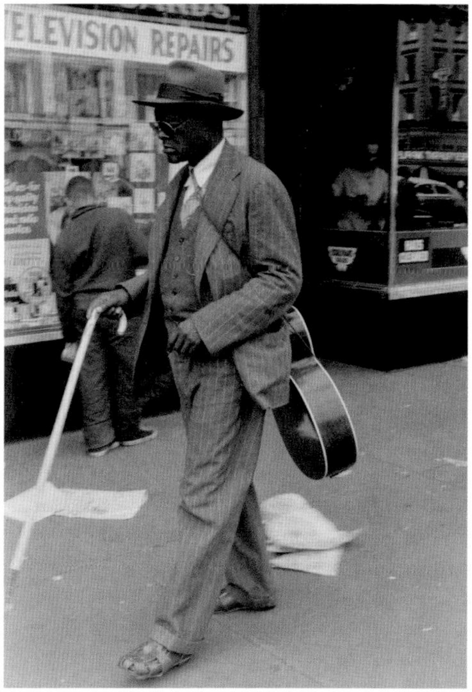
TELEVISION REPAIRS

John Cohen WALKING in THE LIGHT

Steidl

"I LIKES BLUES MUSIC AND GOSPEL:
THEY'VE GOT FEELINGS."

Janie Hunter, Johns Island, South Carolina

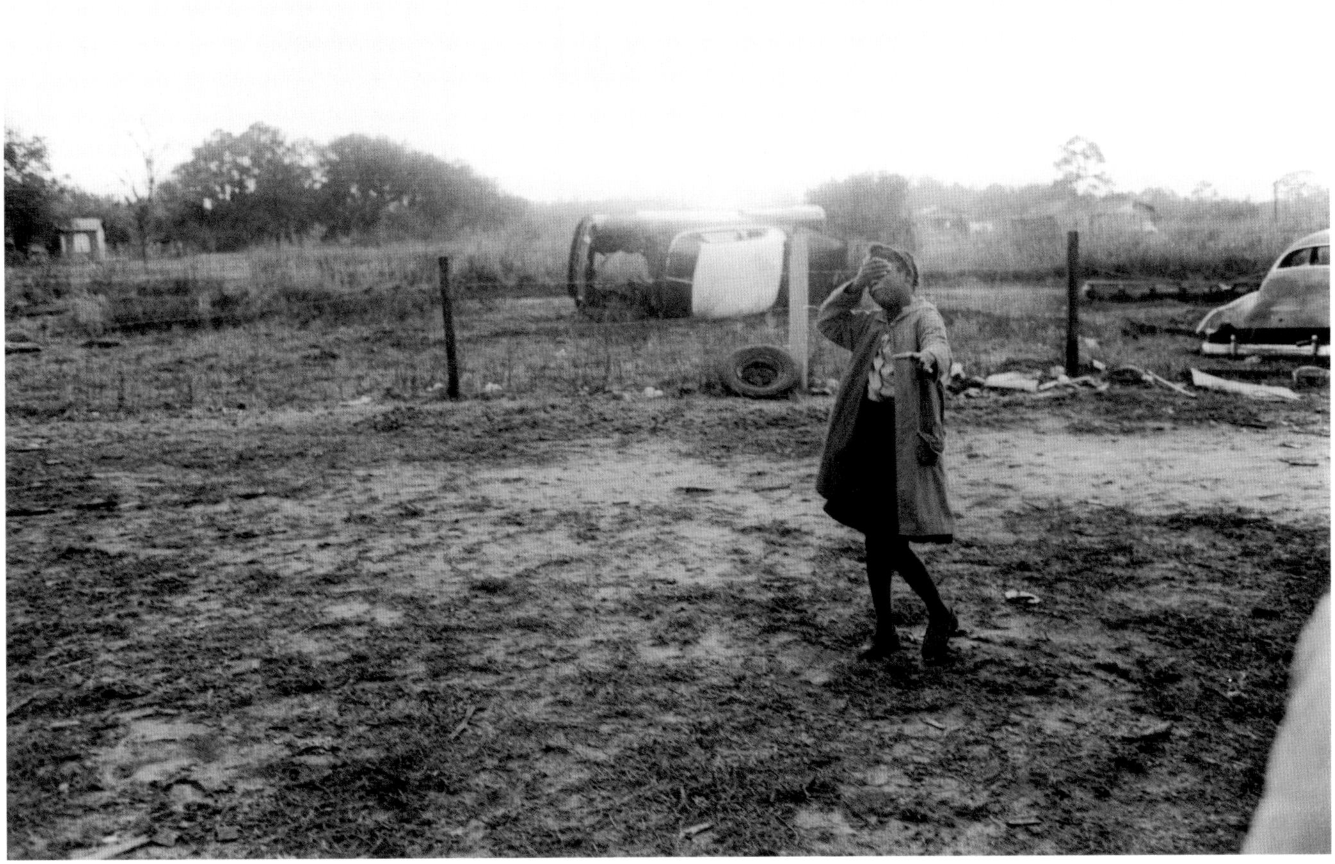

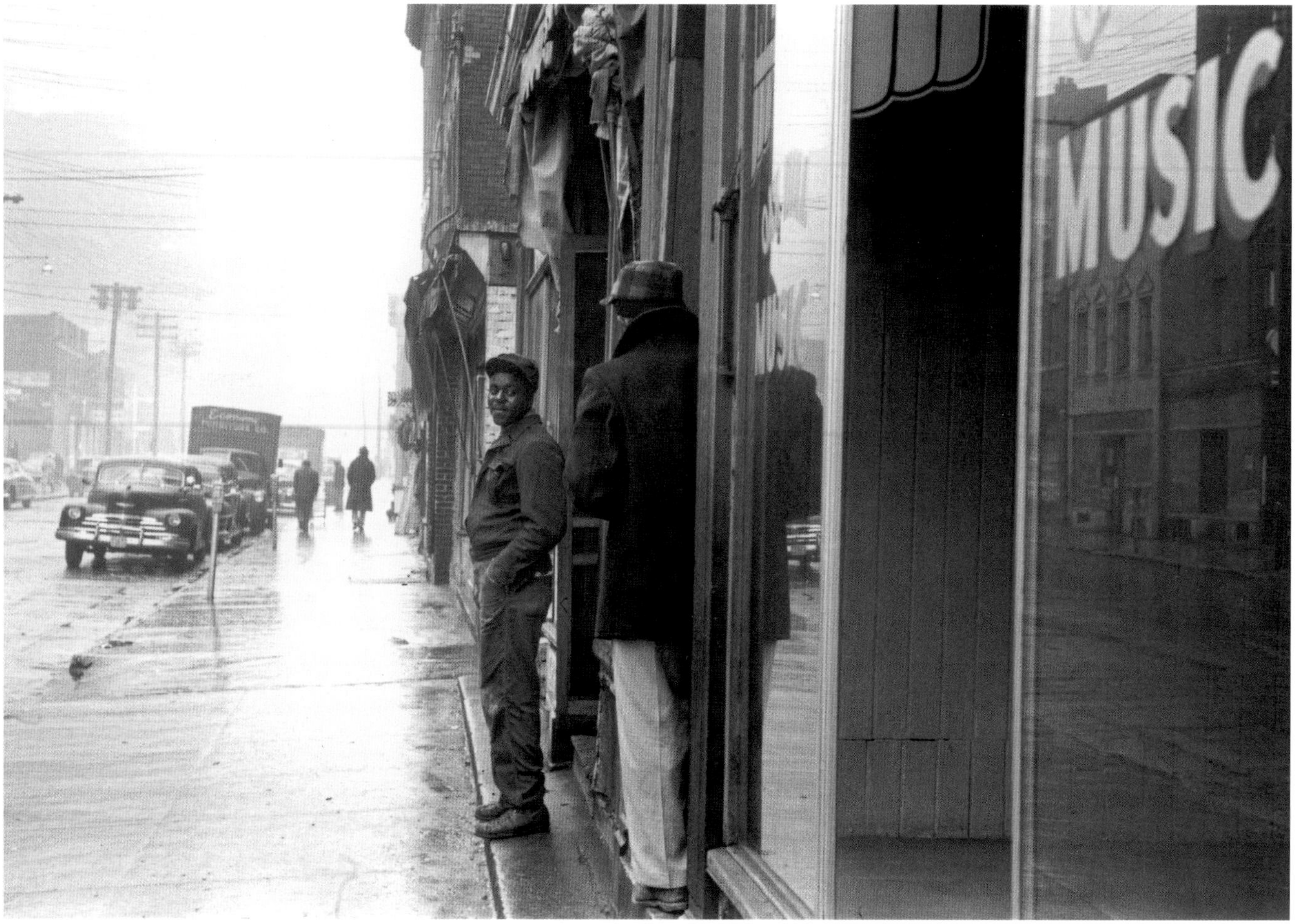
MUSIC

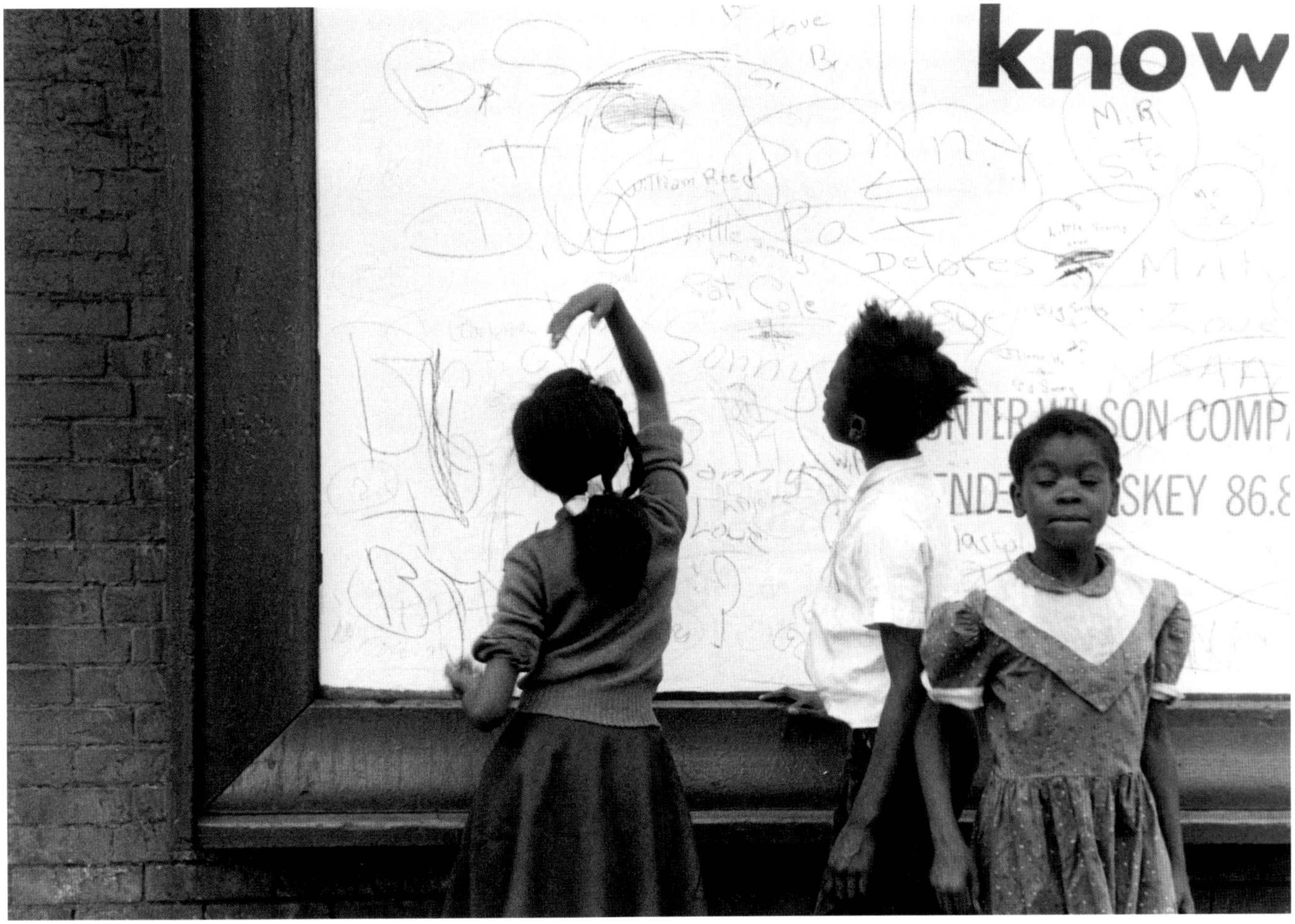
know
NTER WILSON COMP
SKEY 86.8

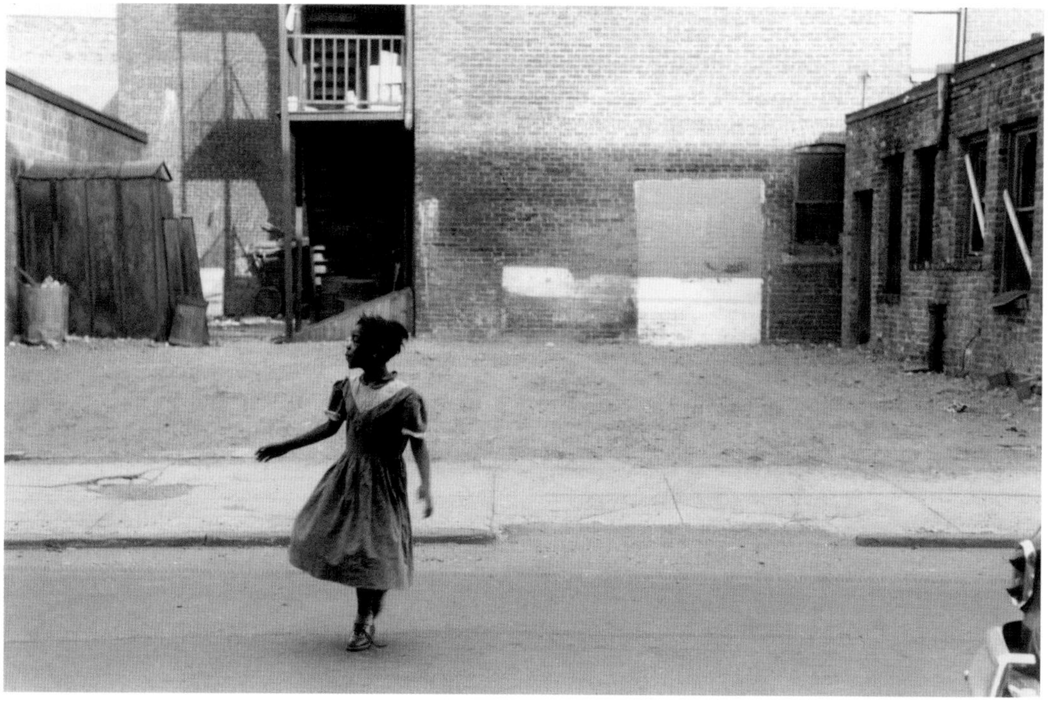

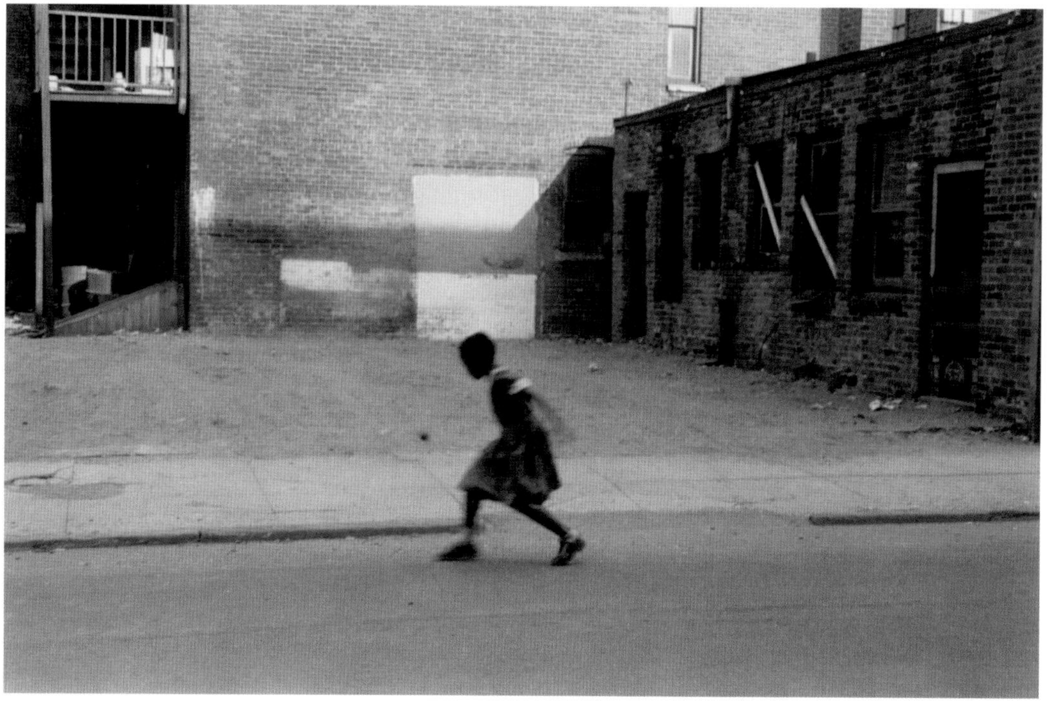

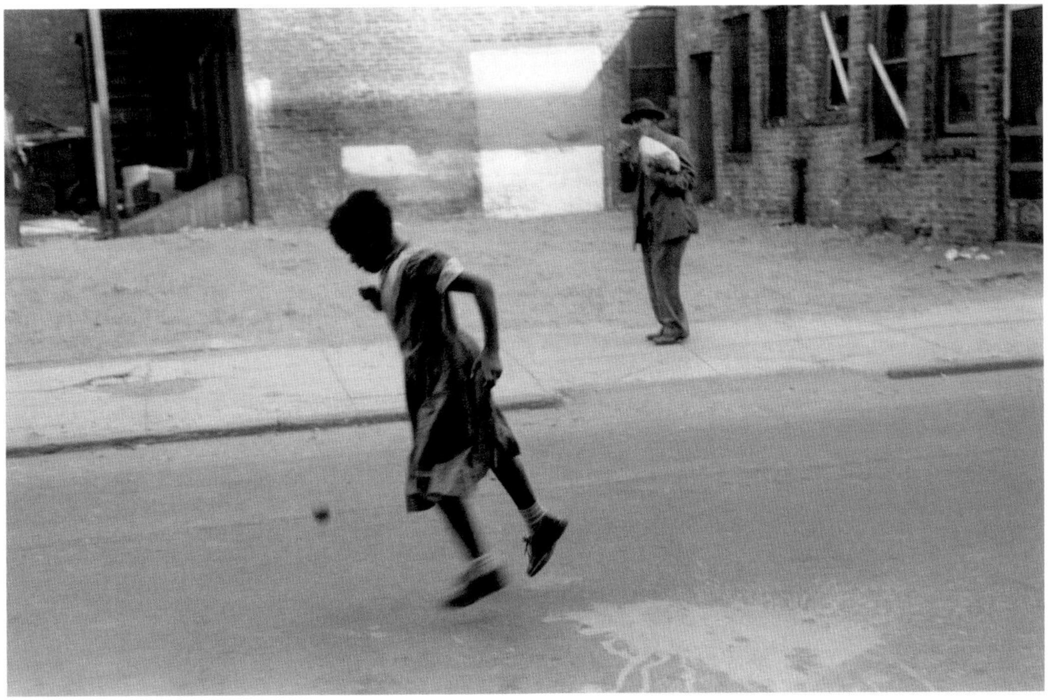

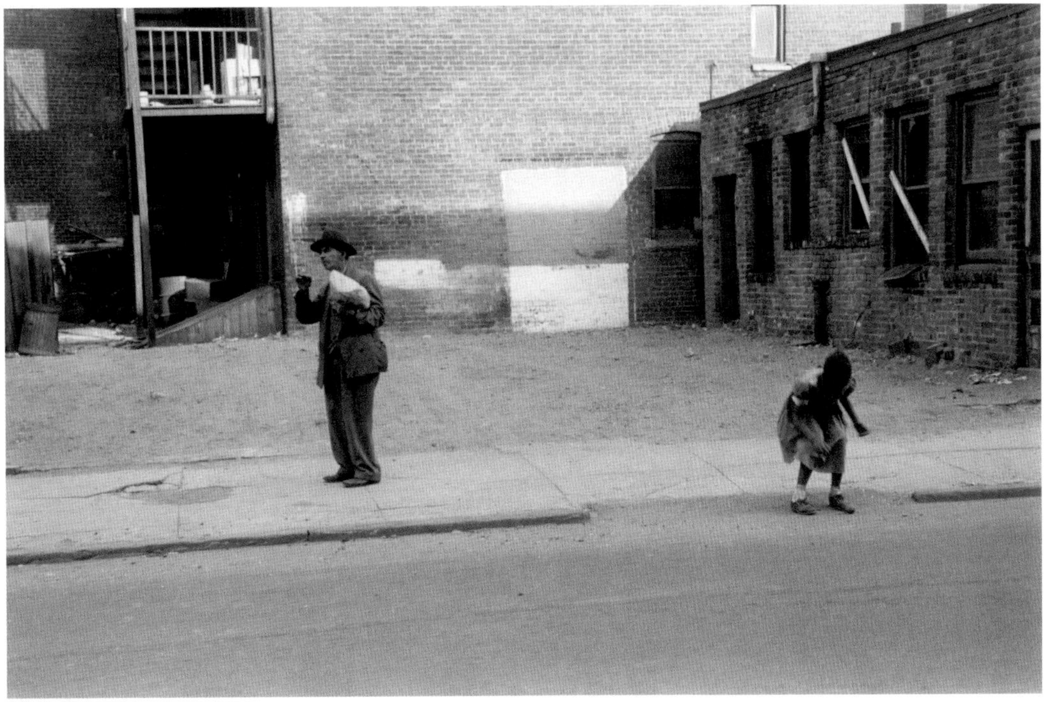

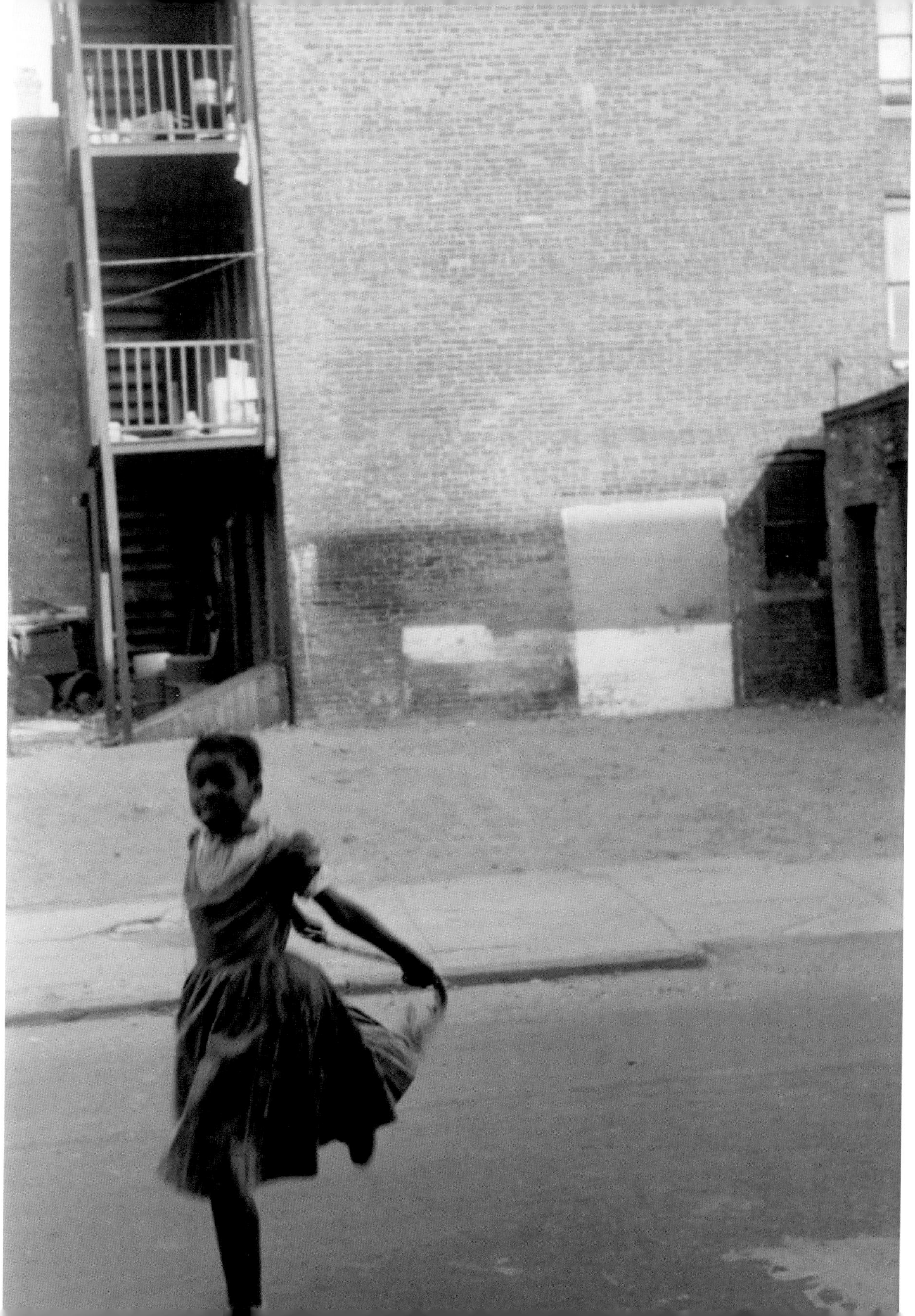

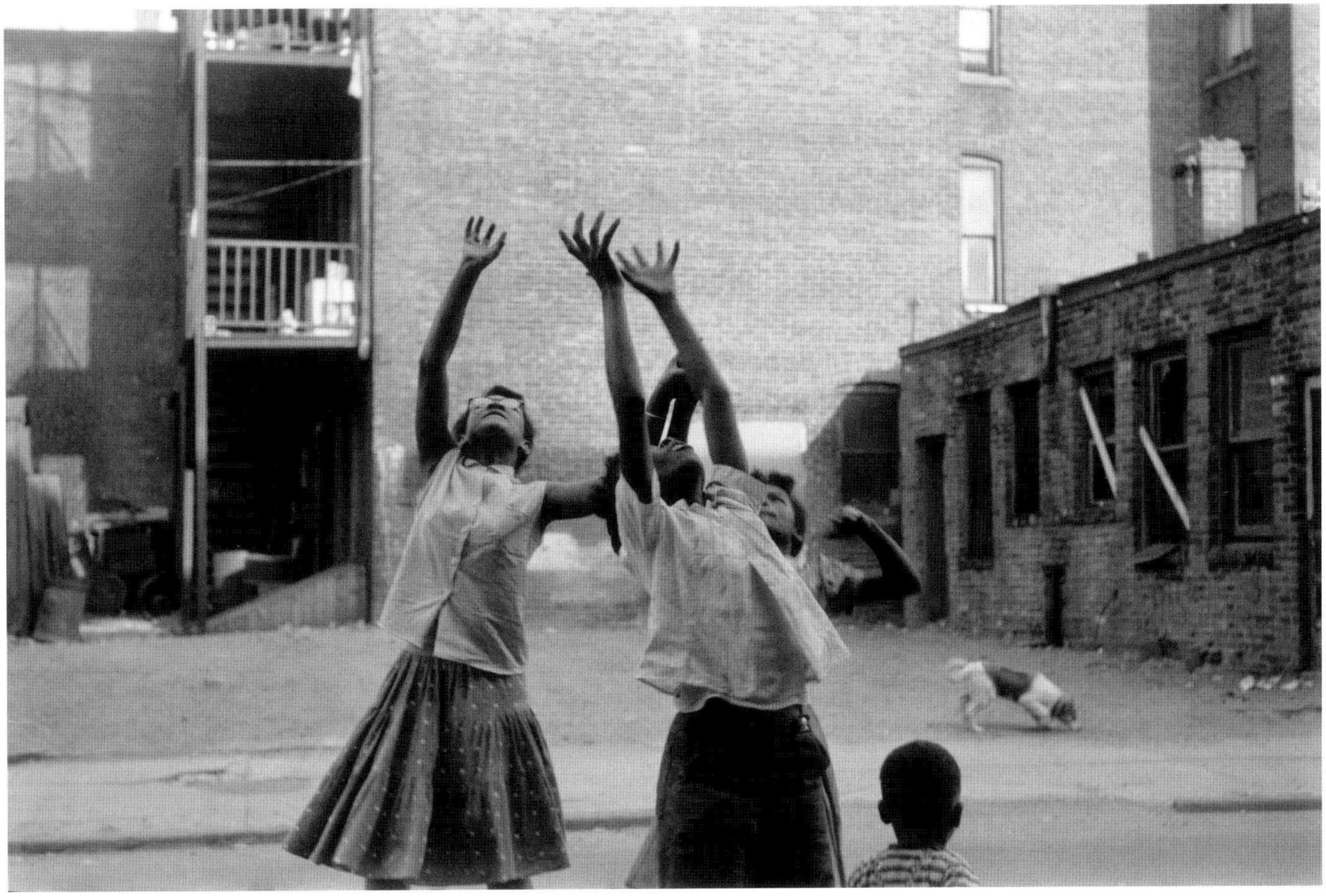

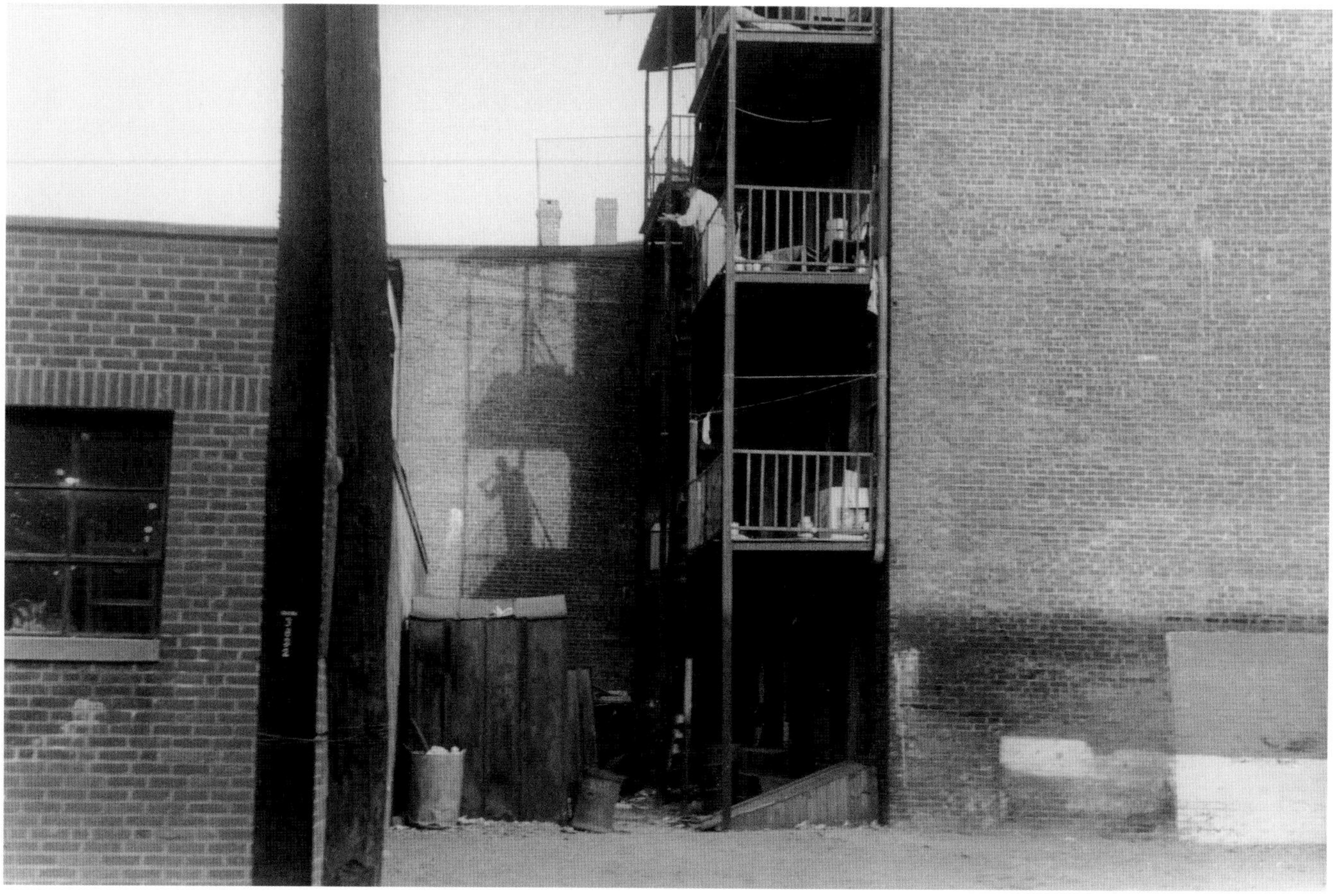

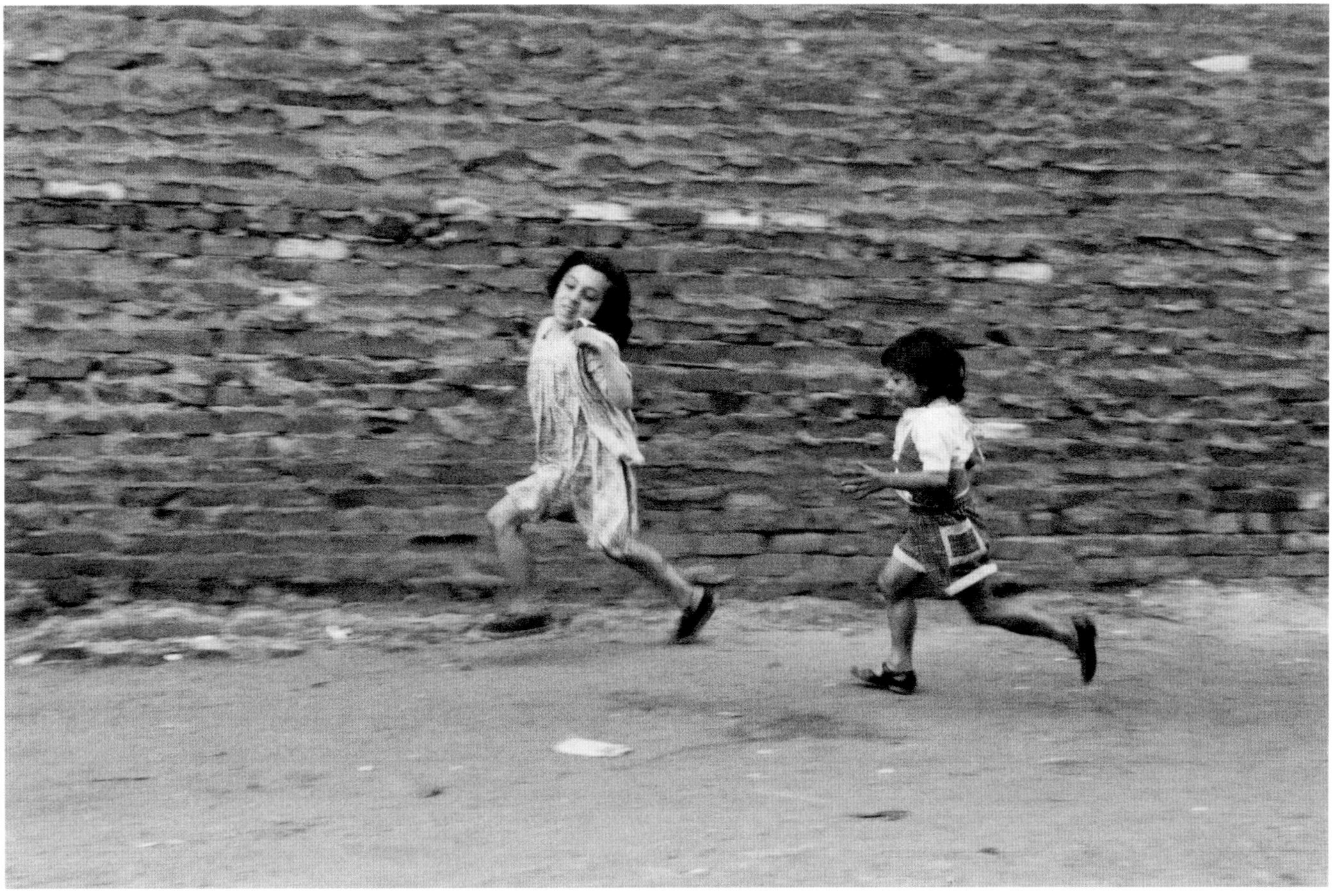

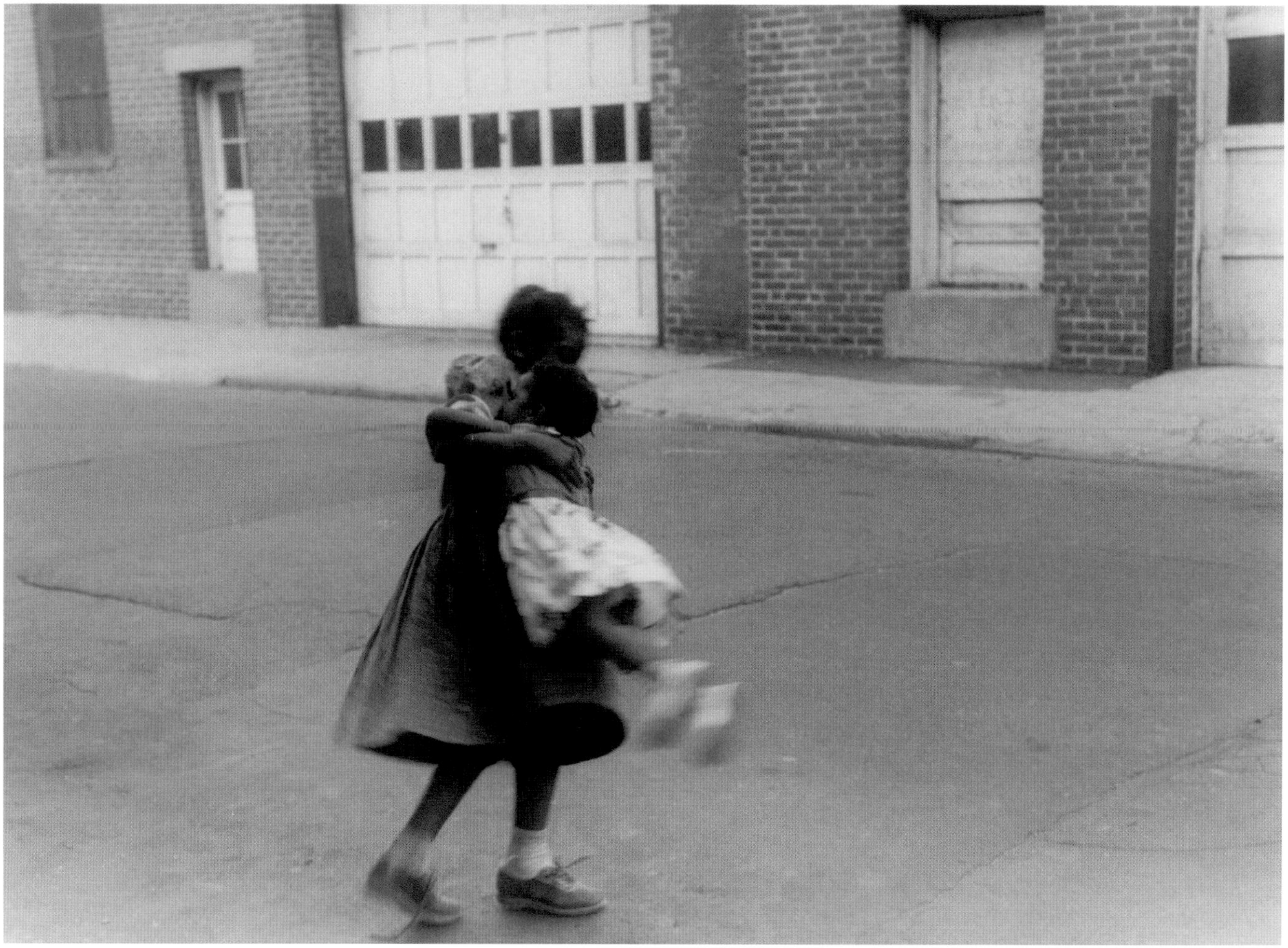

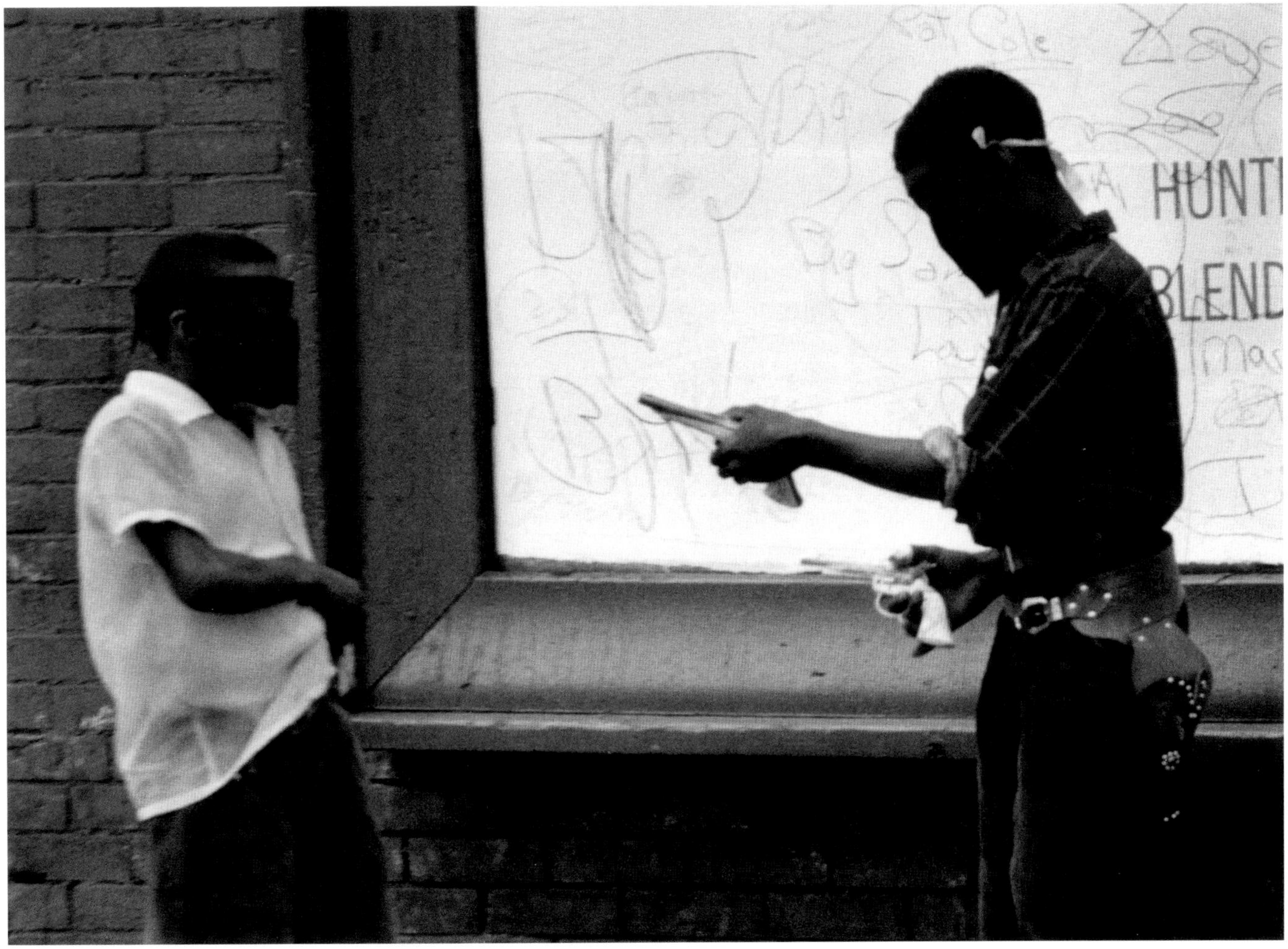
HUNT
BLEND

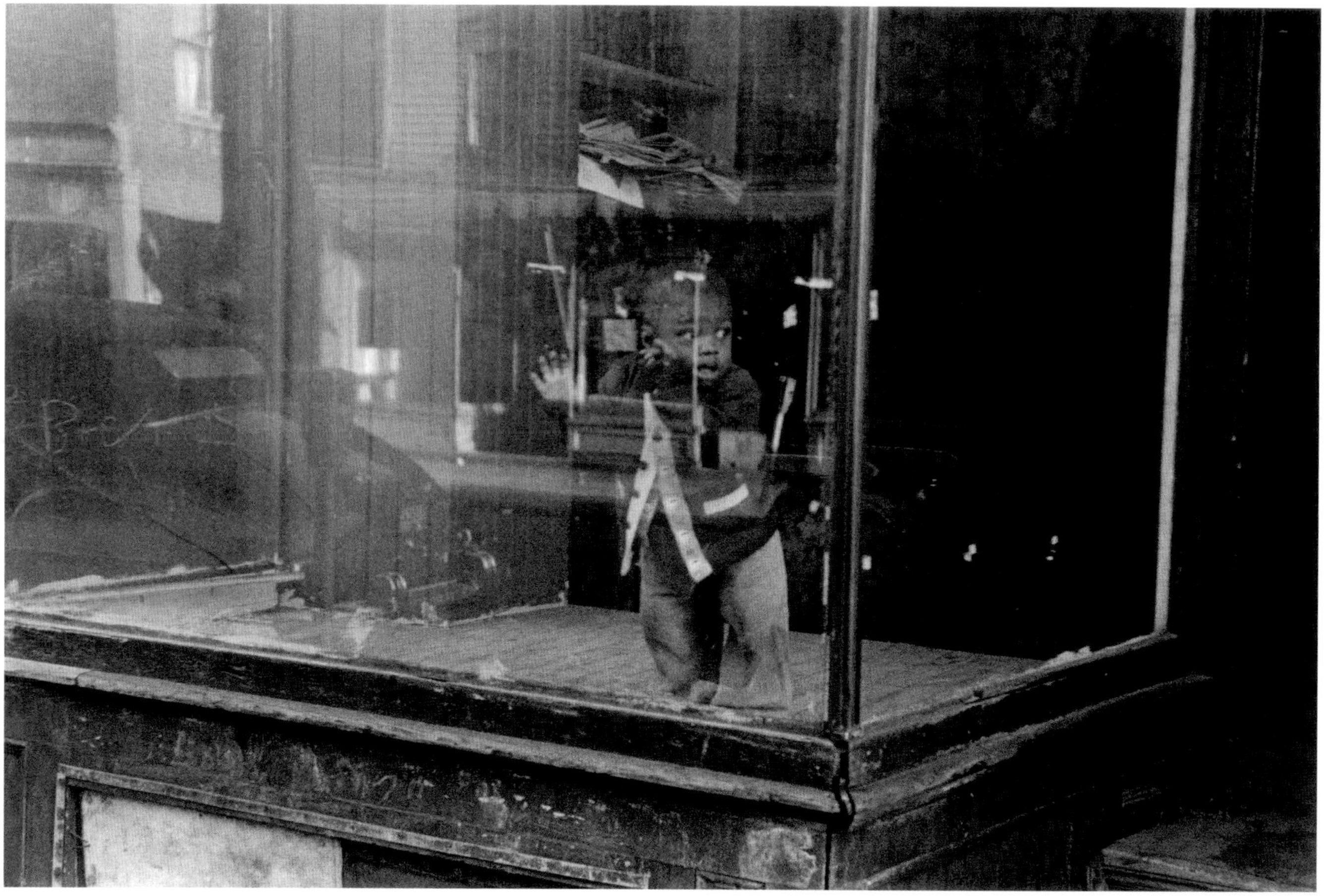

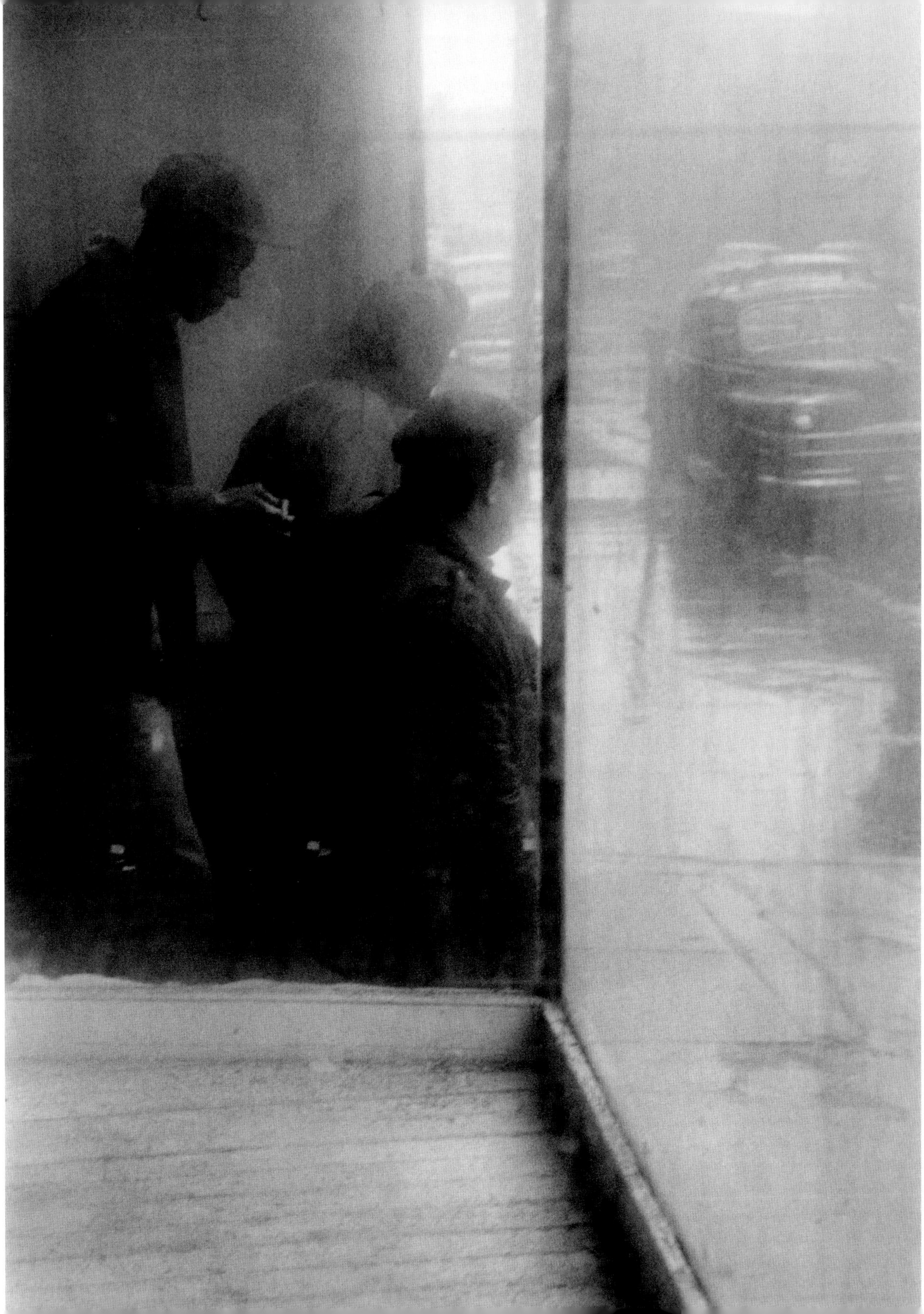

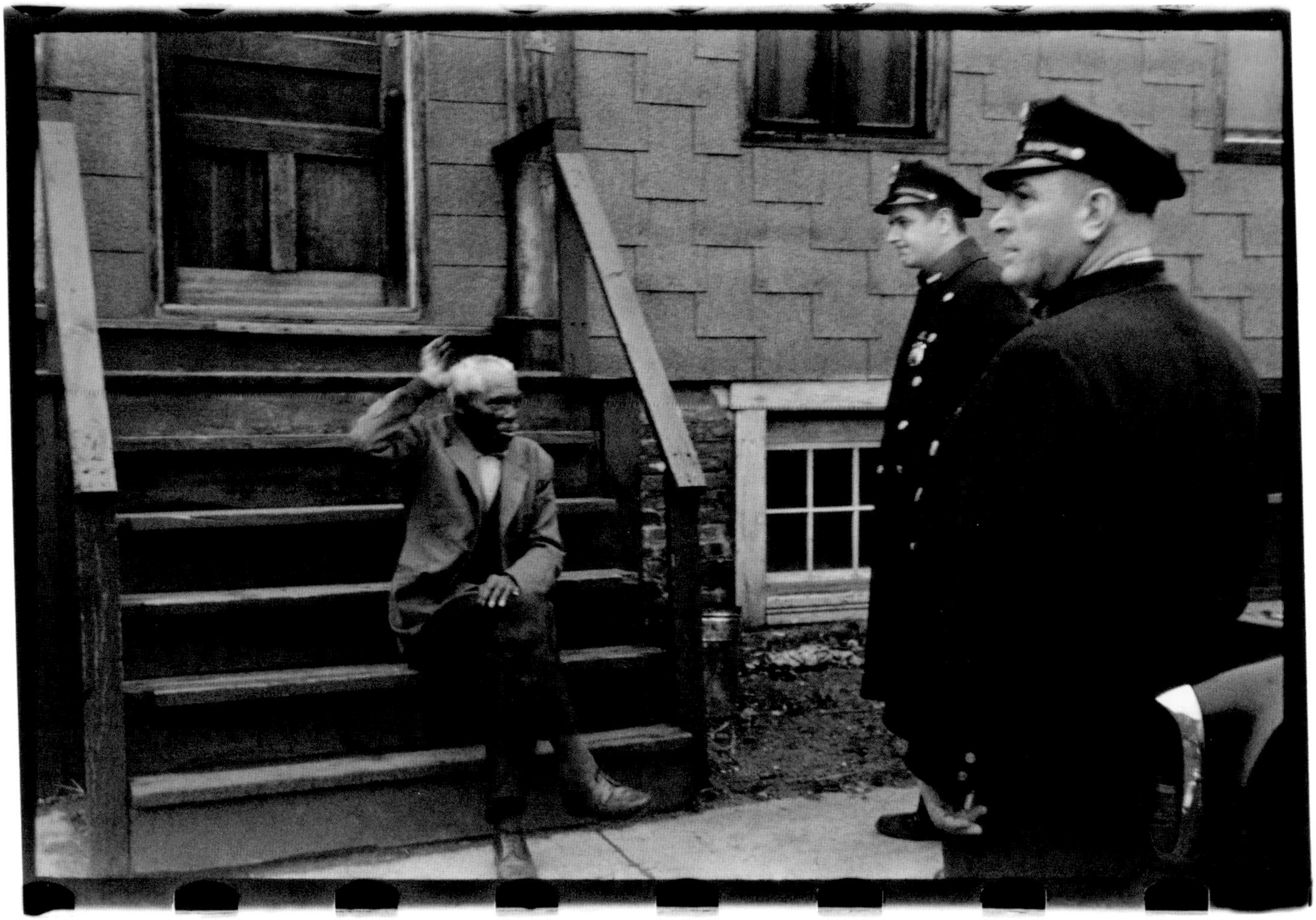

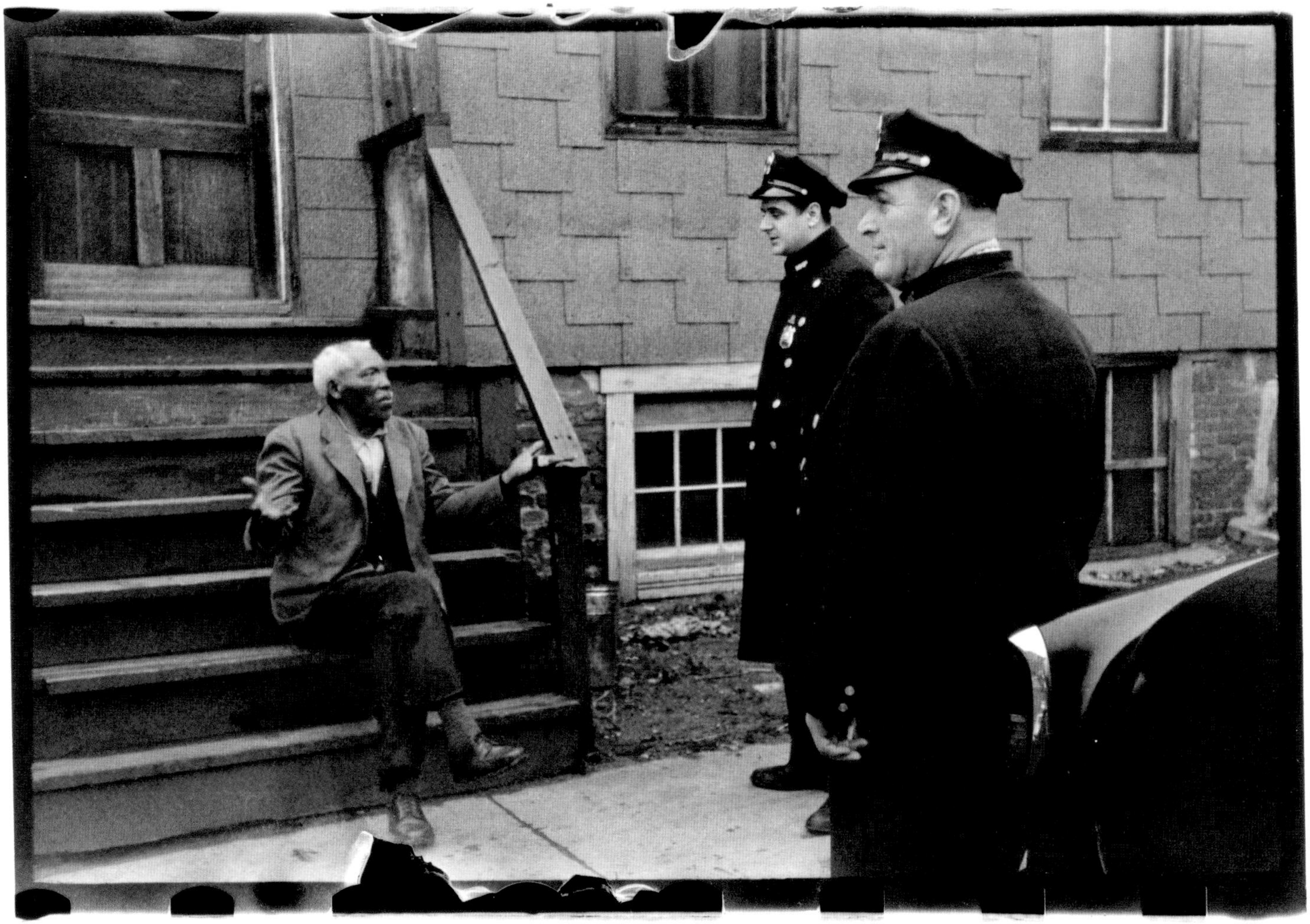

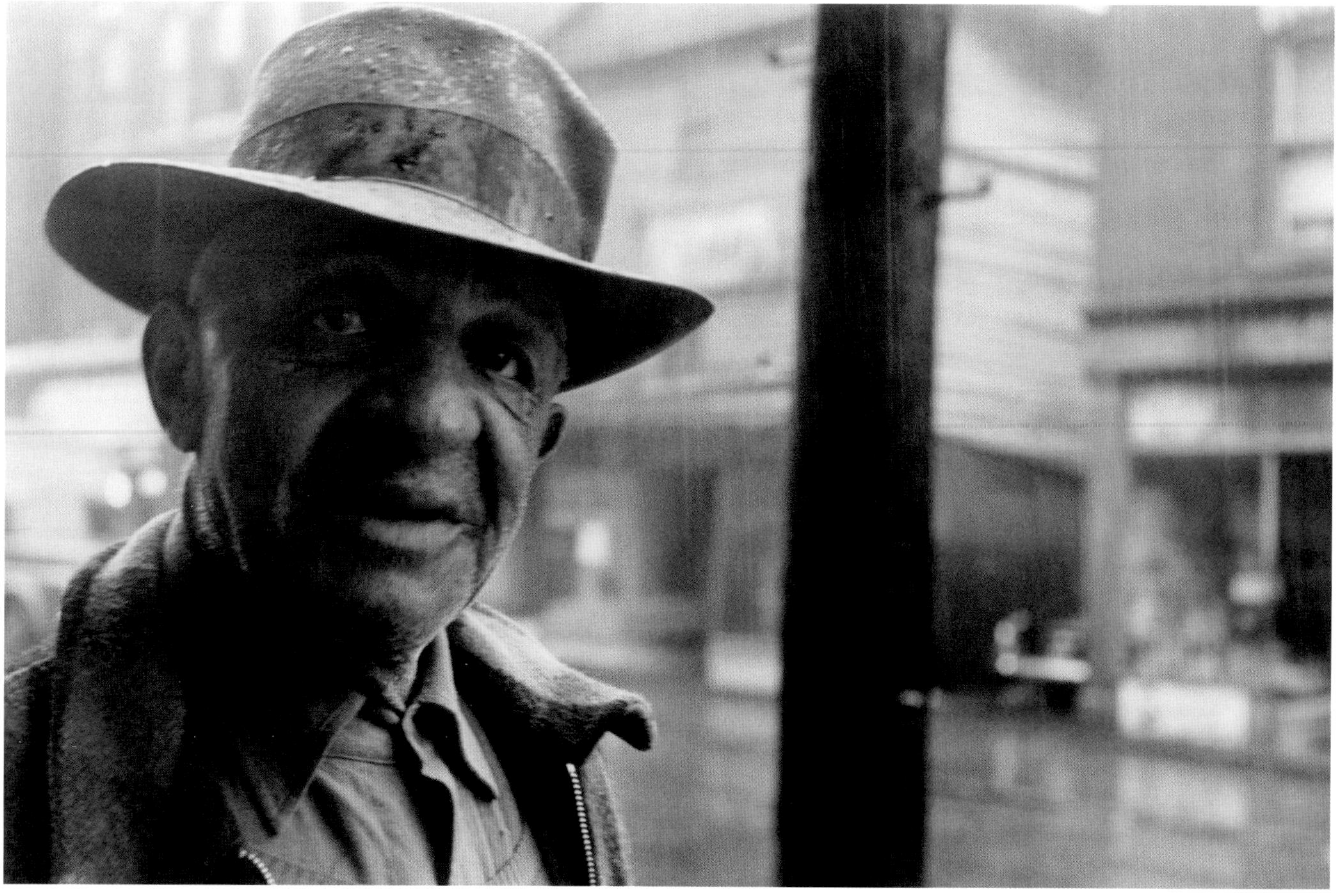

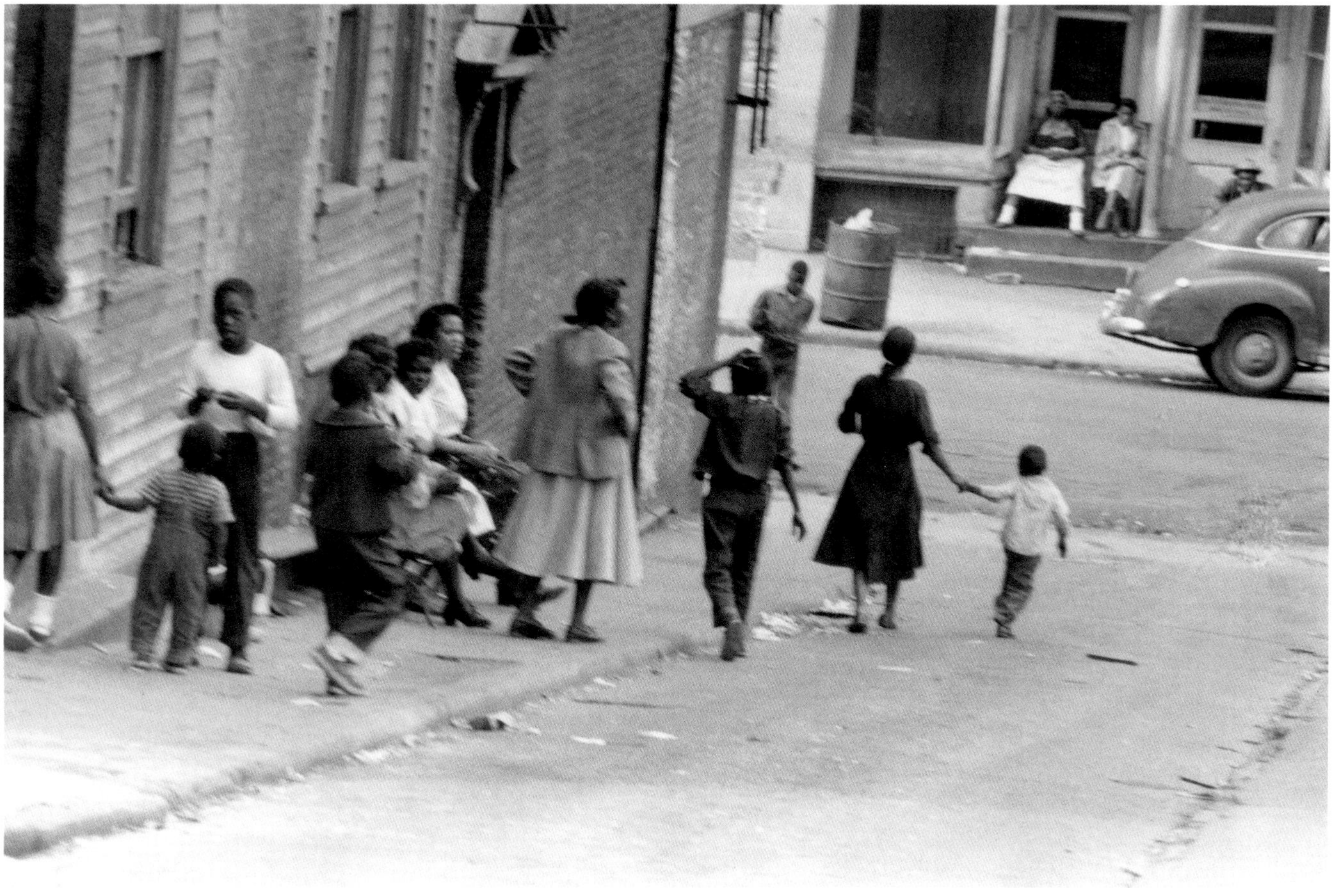

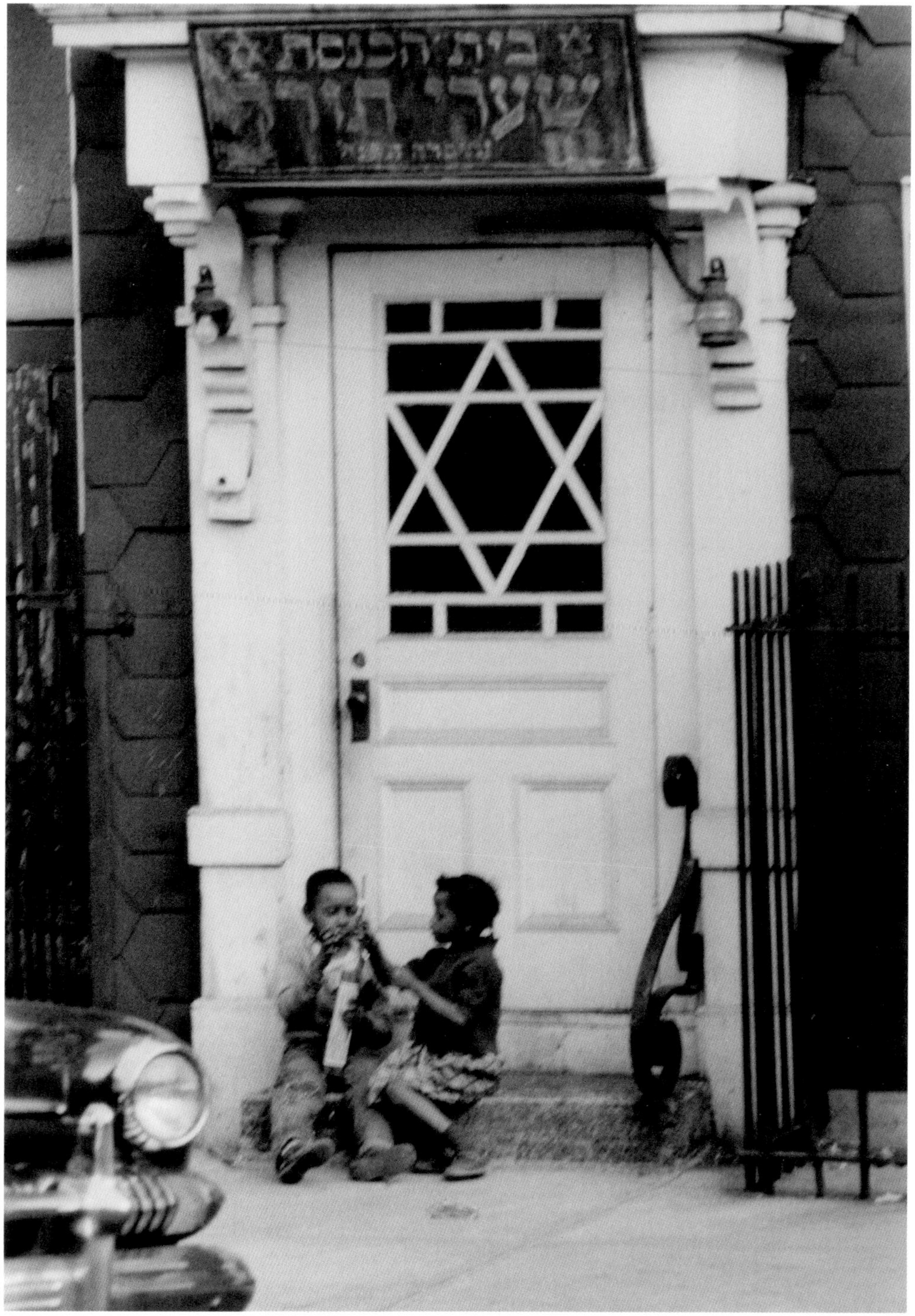
בית הכנסת

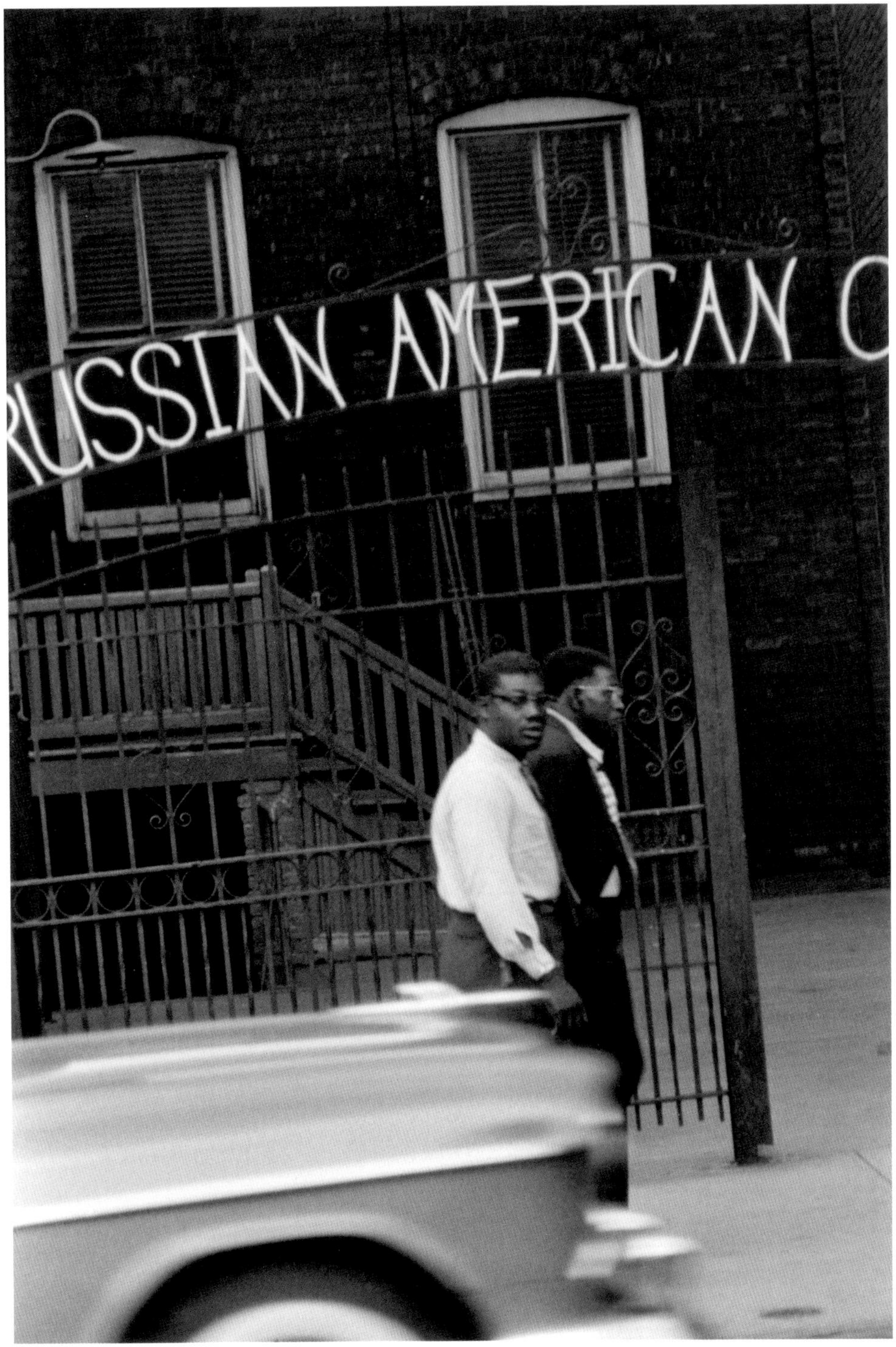
RUSSIAN AMERICAN

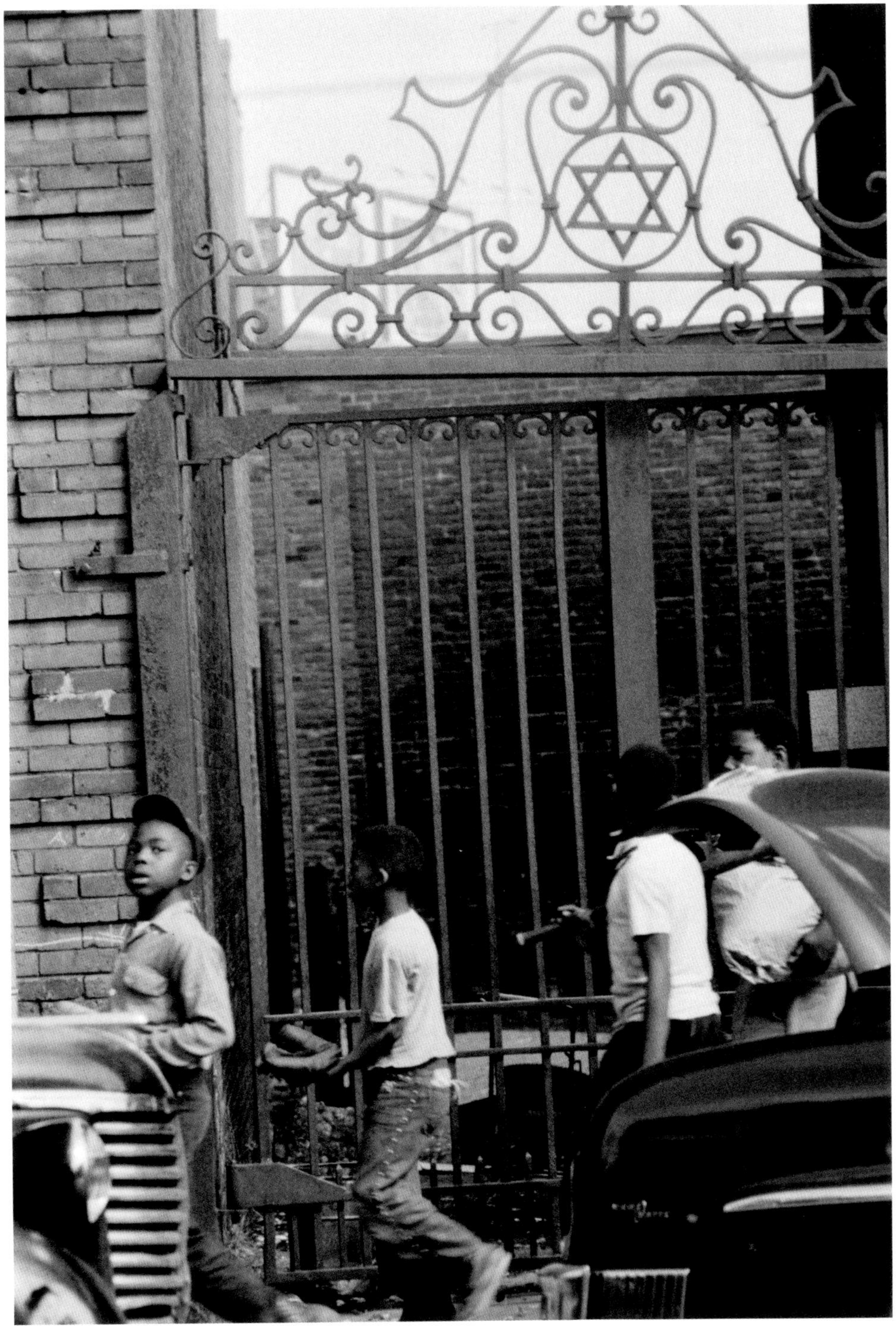

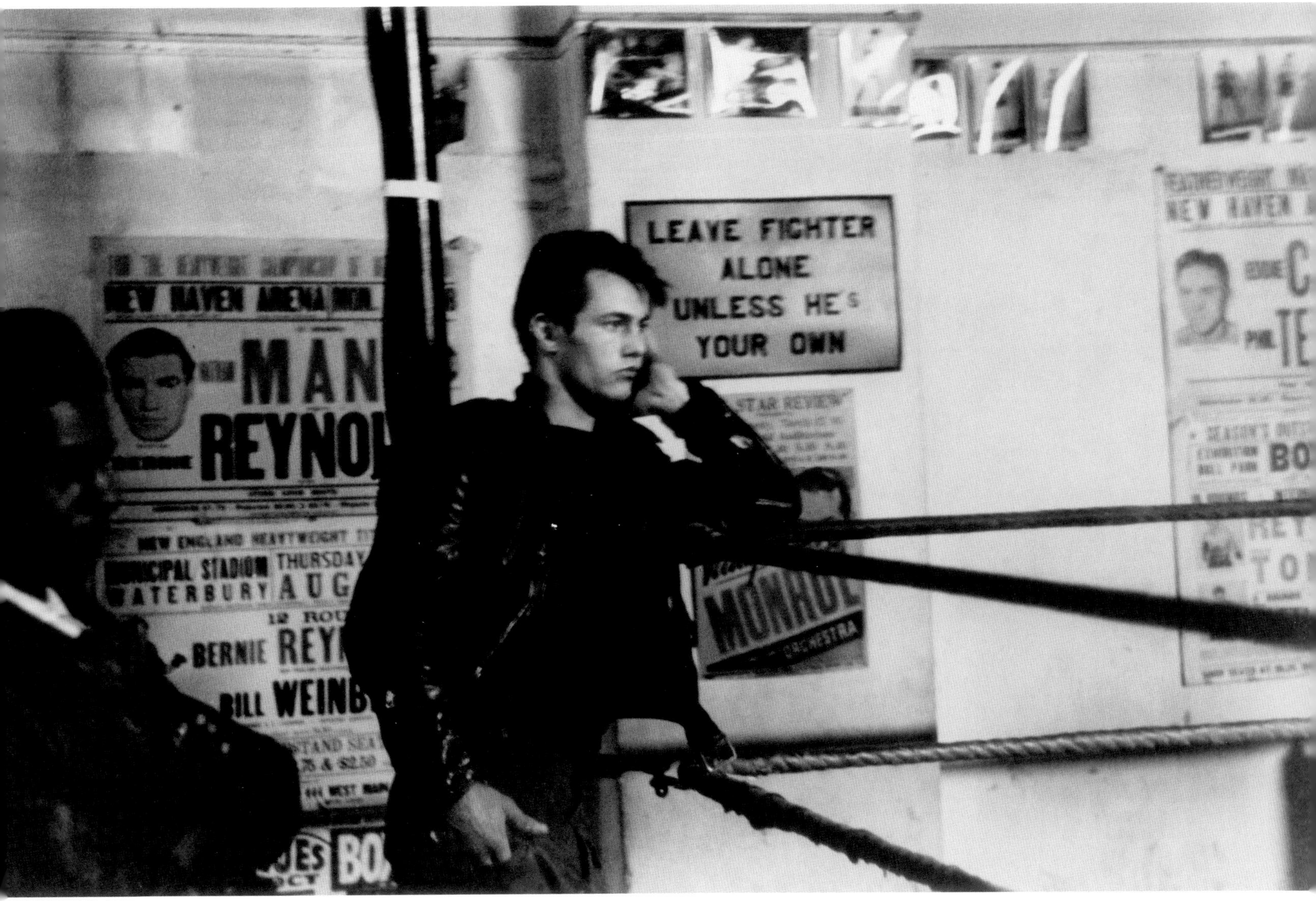
LEAVE FIGHTER
ALONE
UNLESS HE'S
YOUR OWN
NEW HAVEN ARENA
THURSDAY
WATERBURY
BERNIE
ORCHESTRA

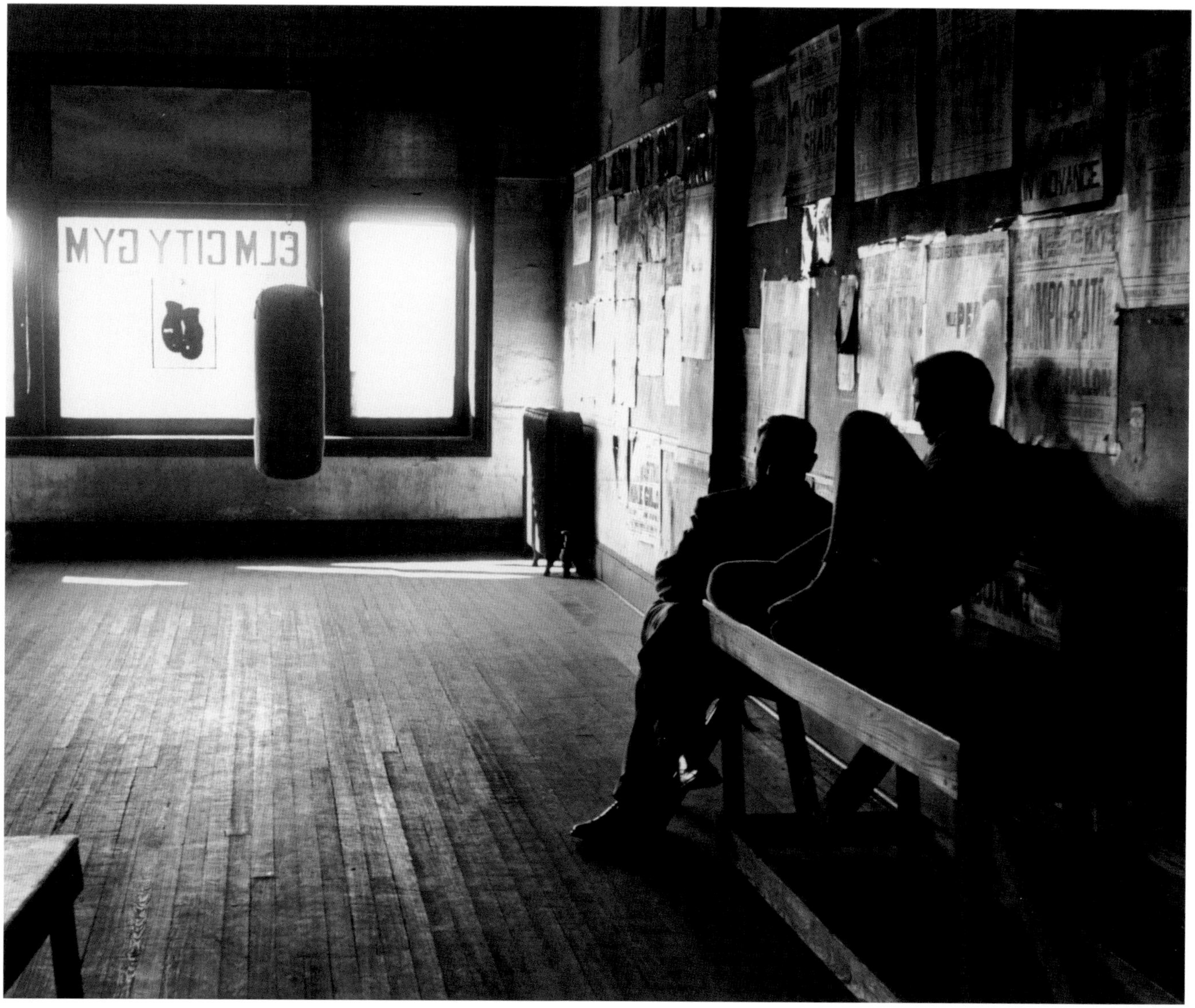
ELM CITY GYM

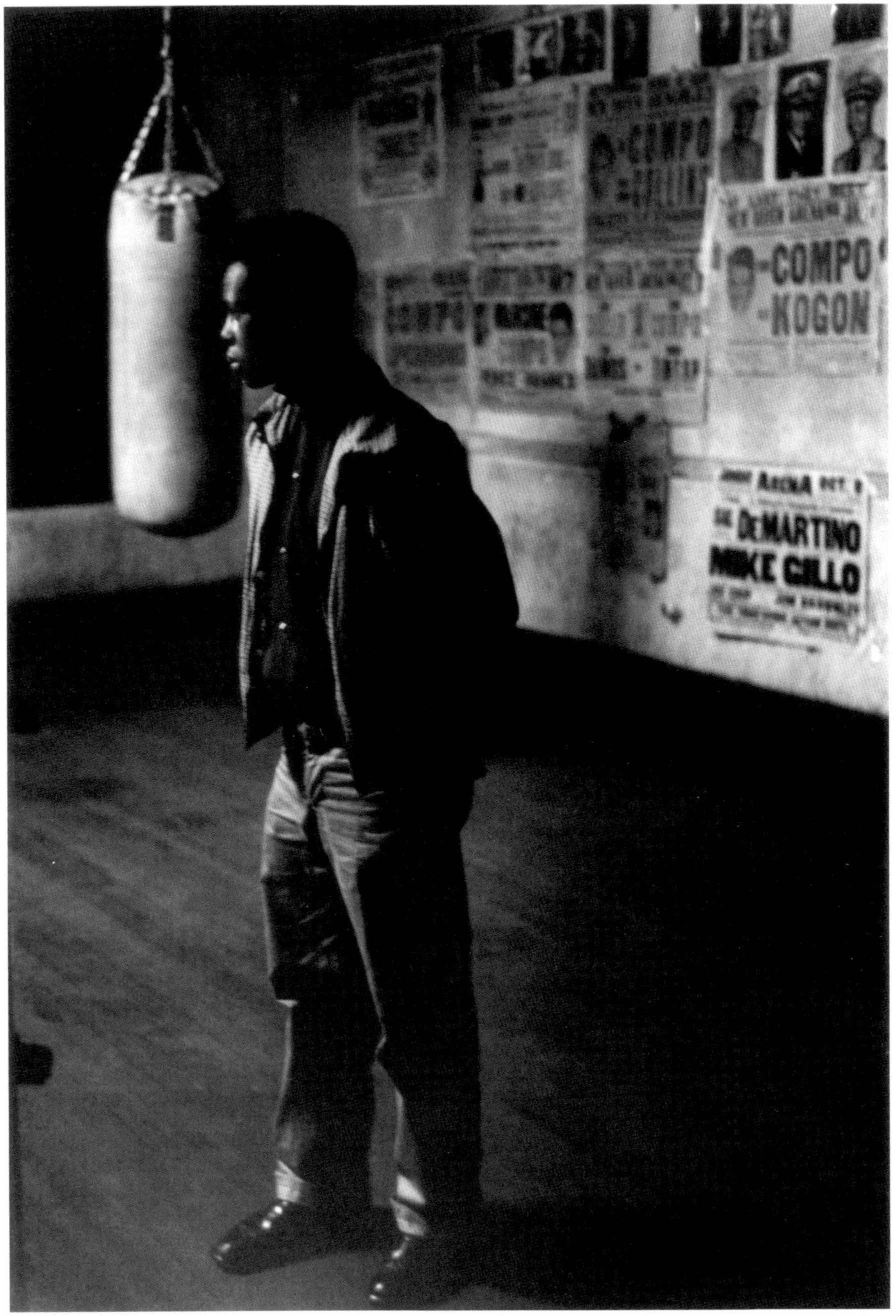
COMPO
KOGON
DeMARTINO
MIKE GILLO

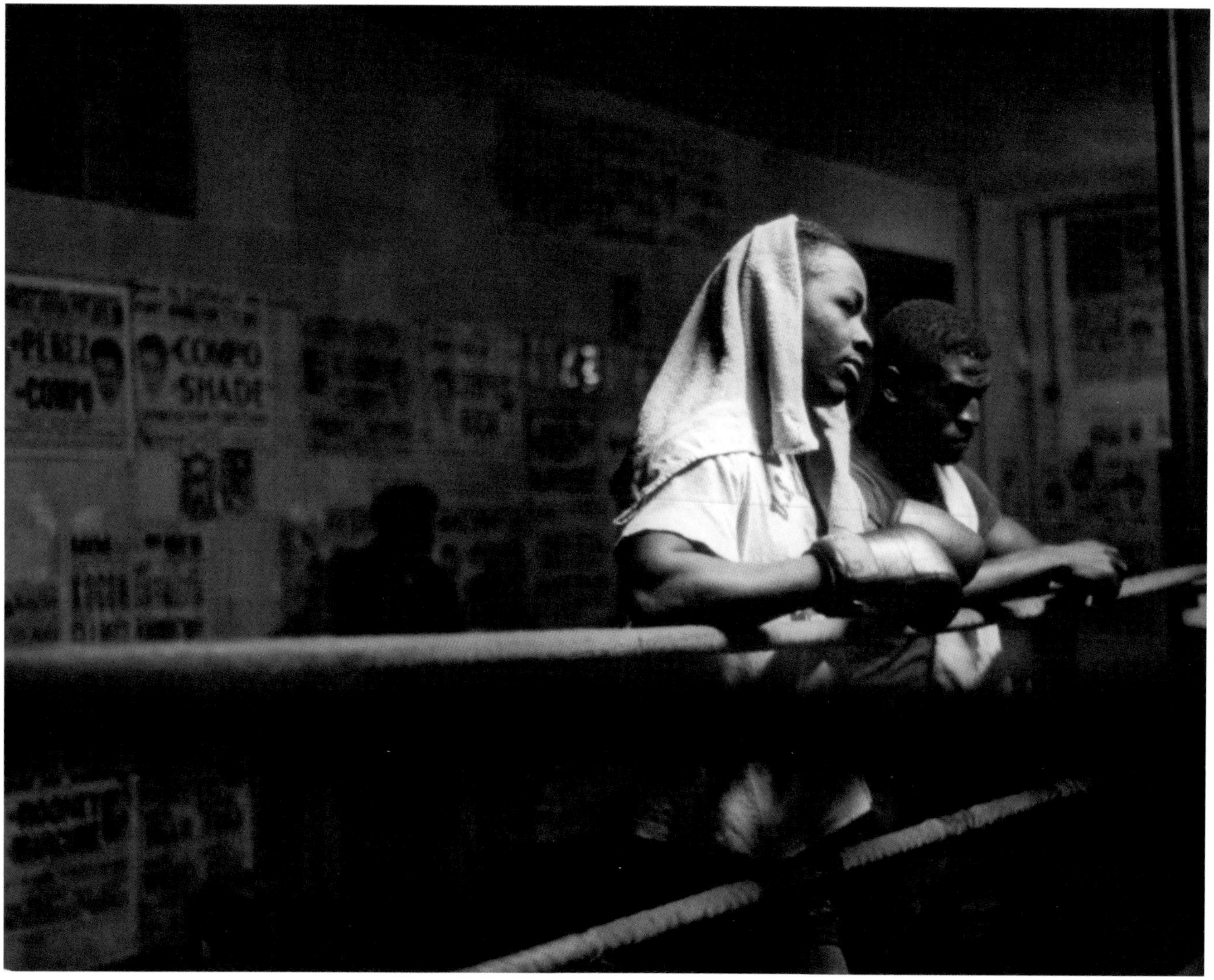

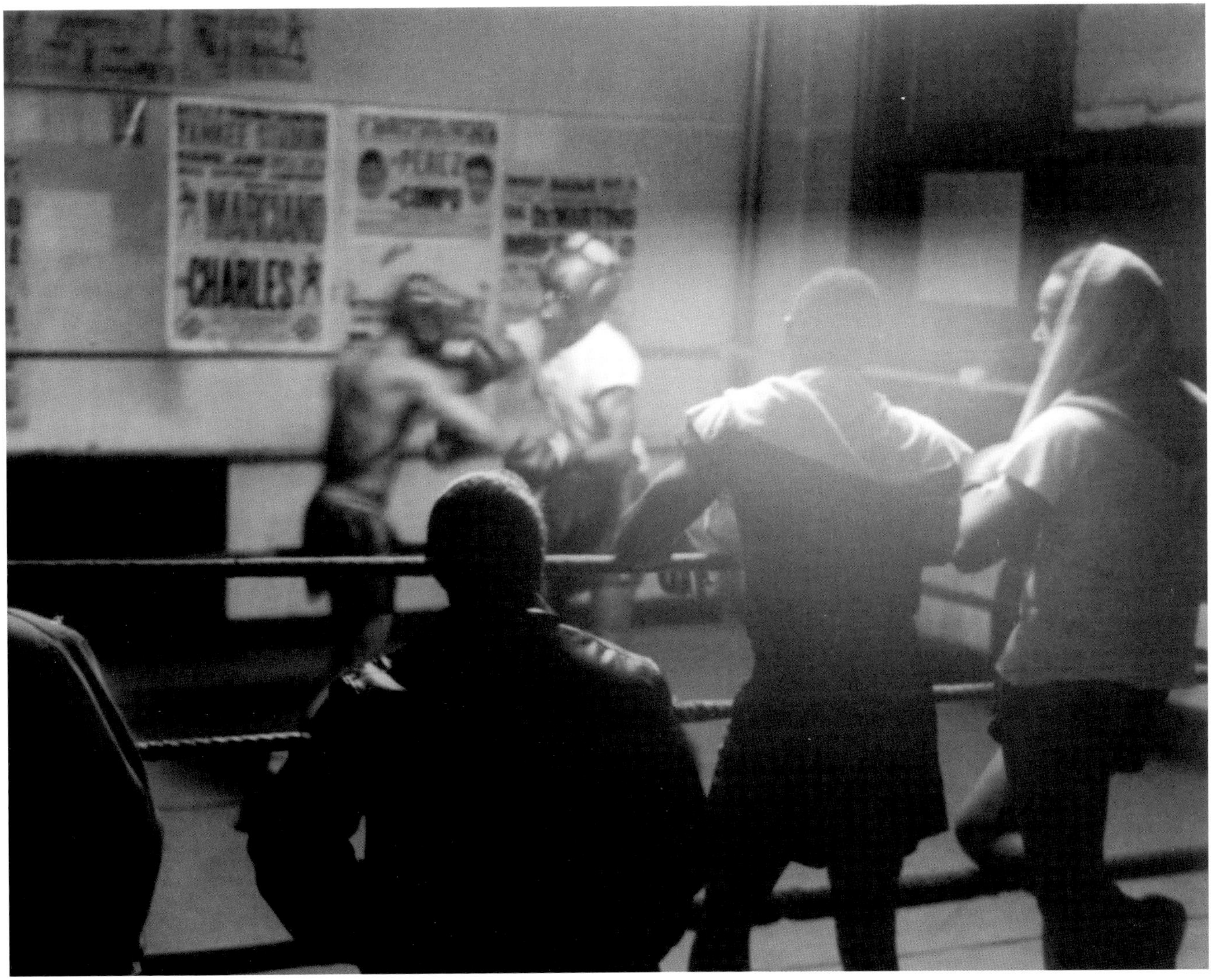
CHARLES

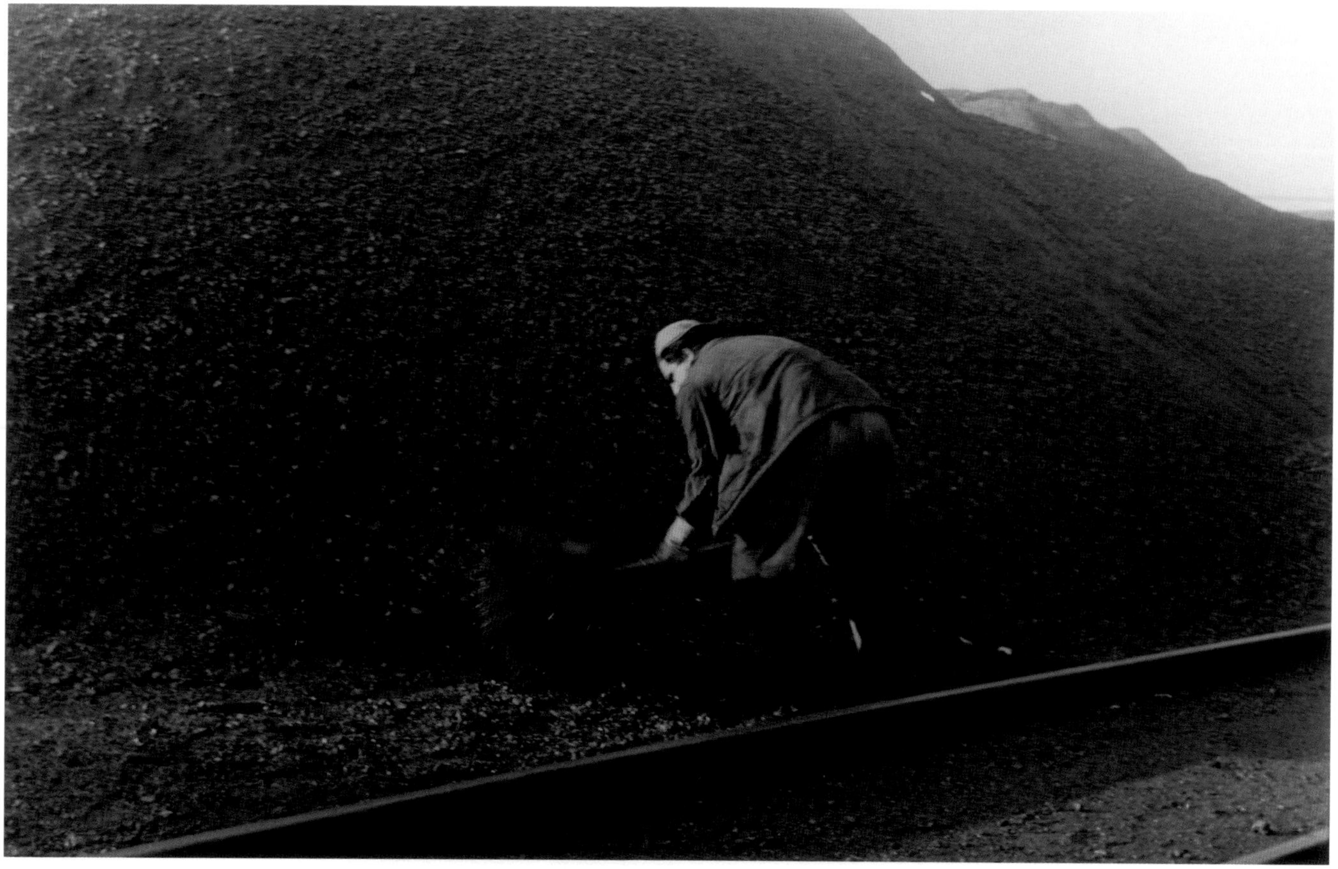

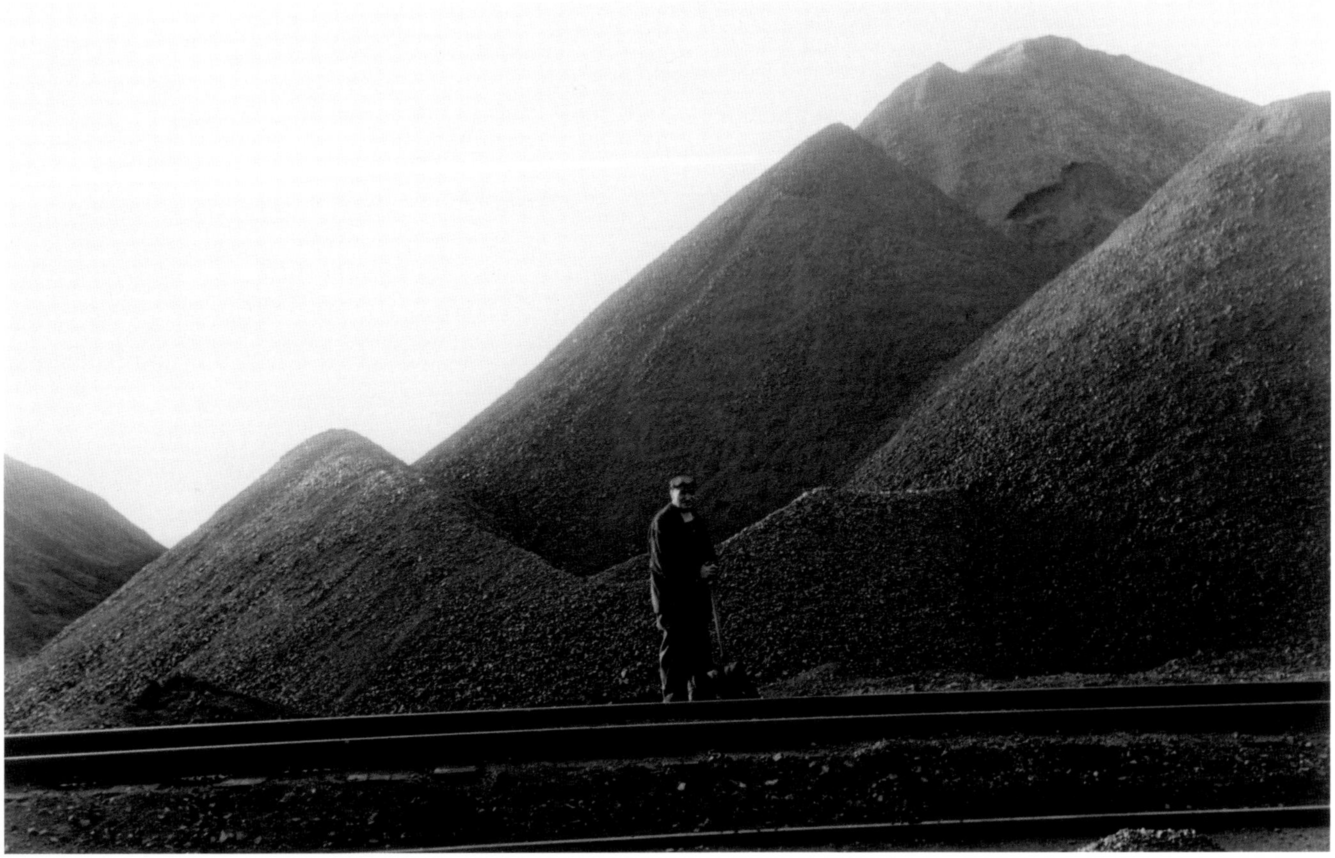

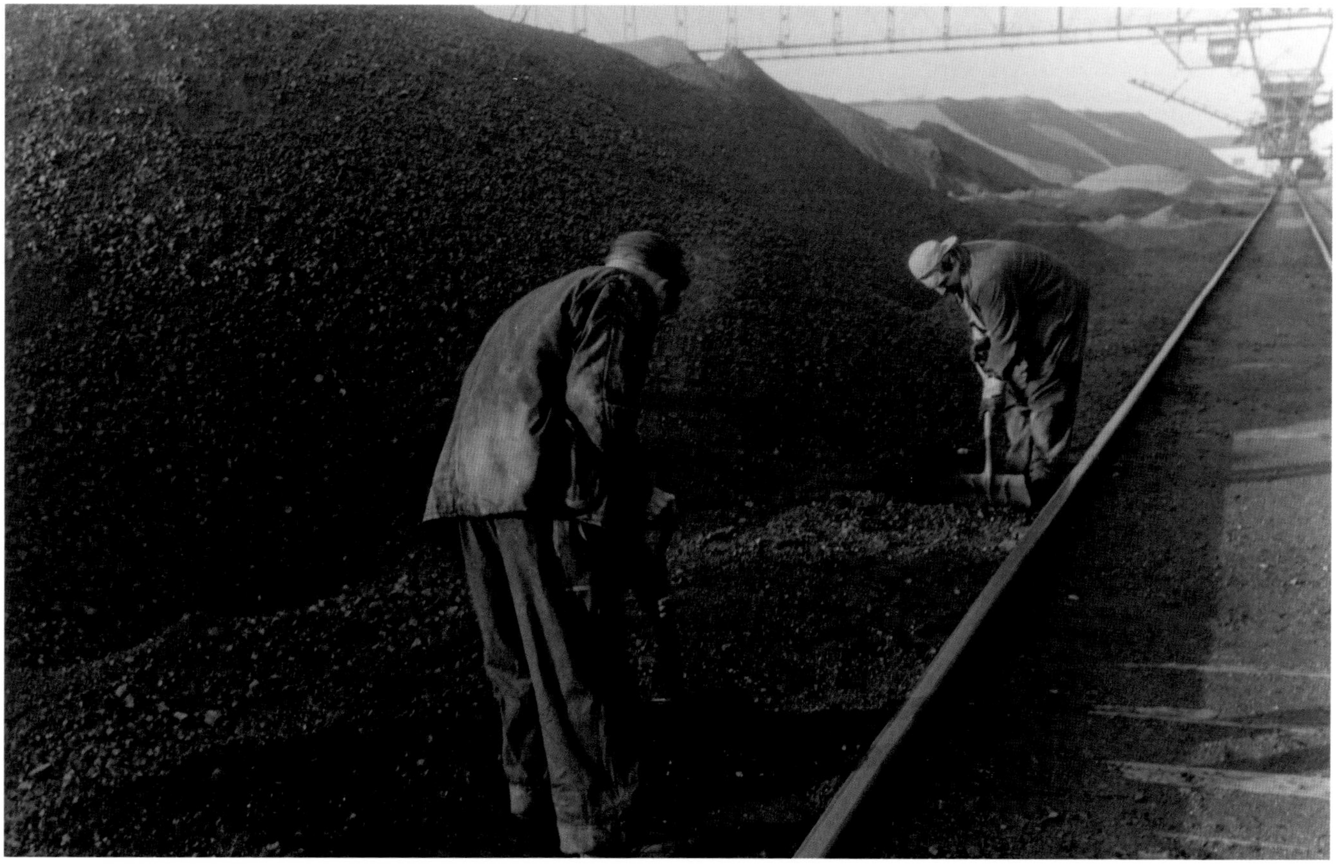

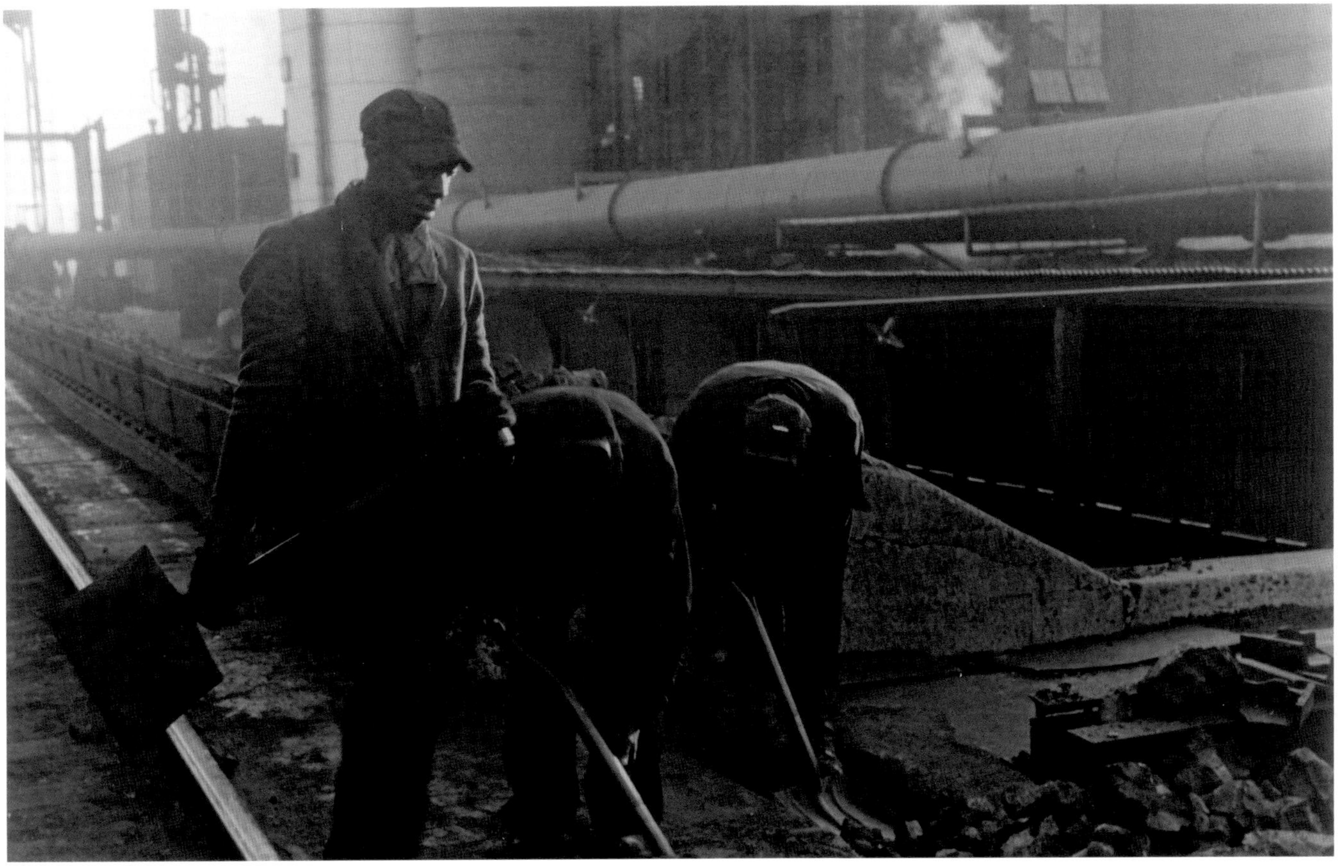

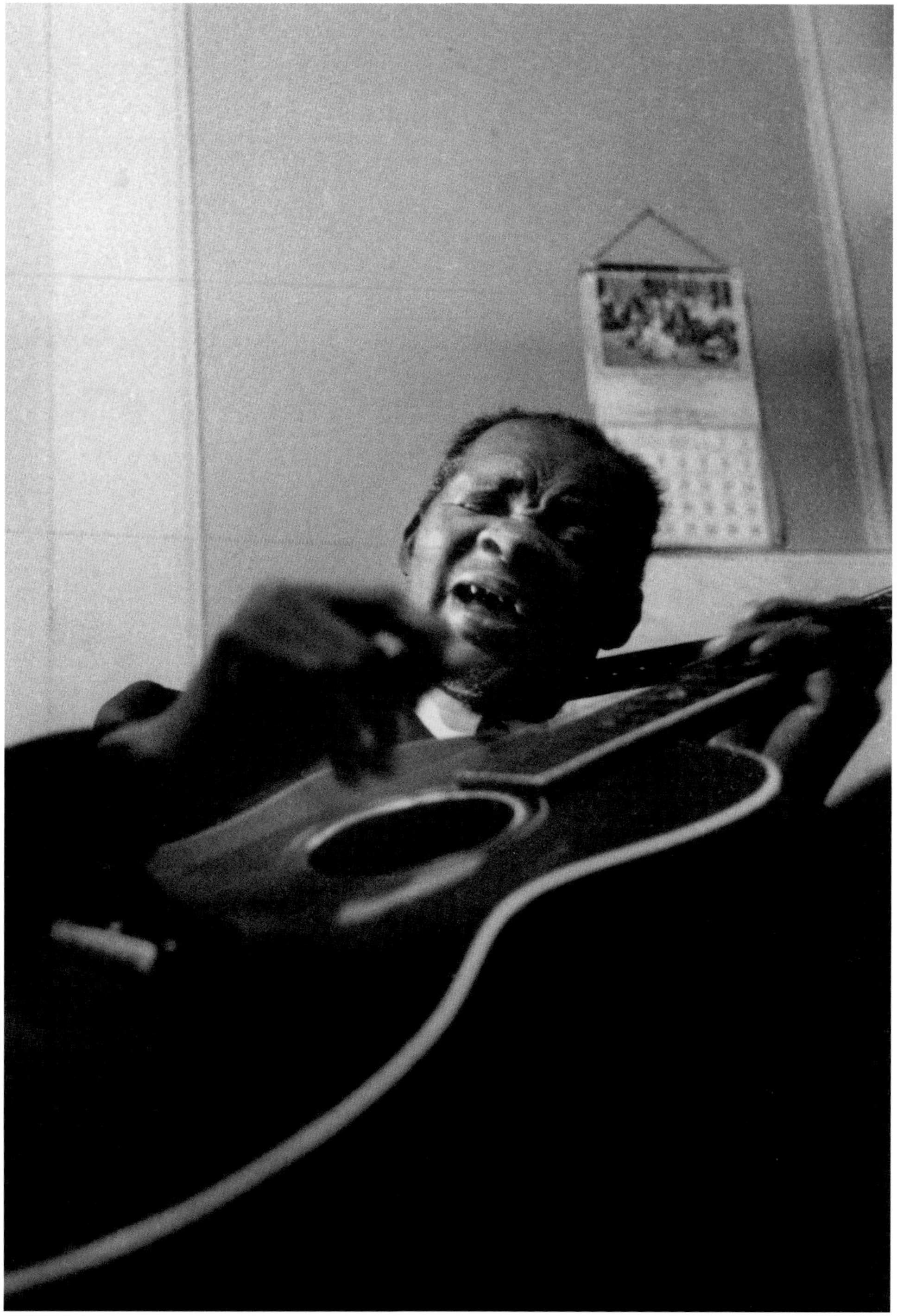

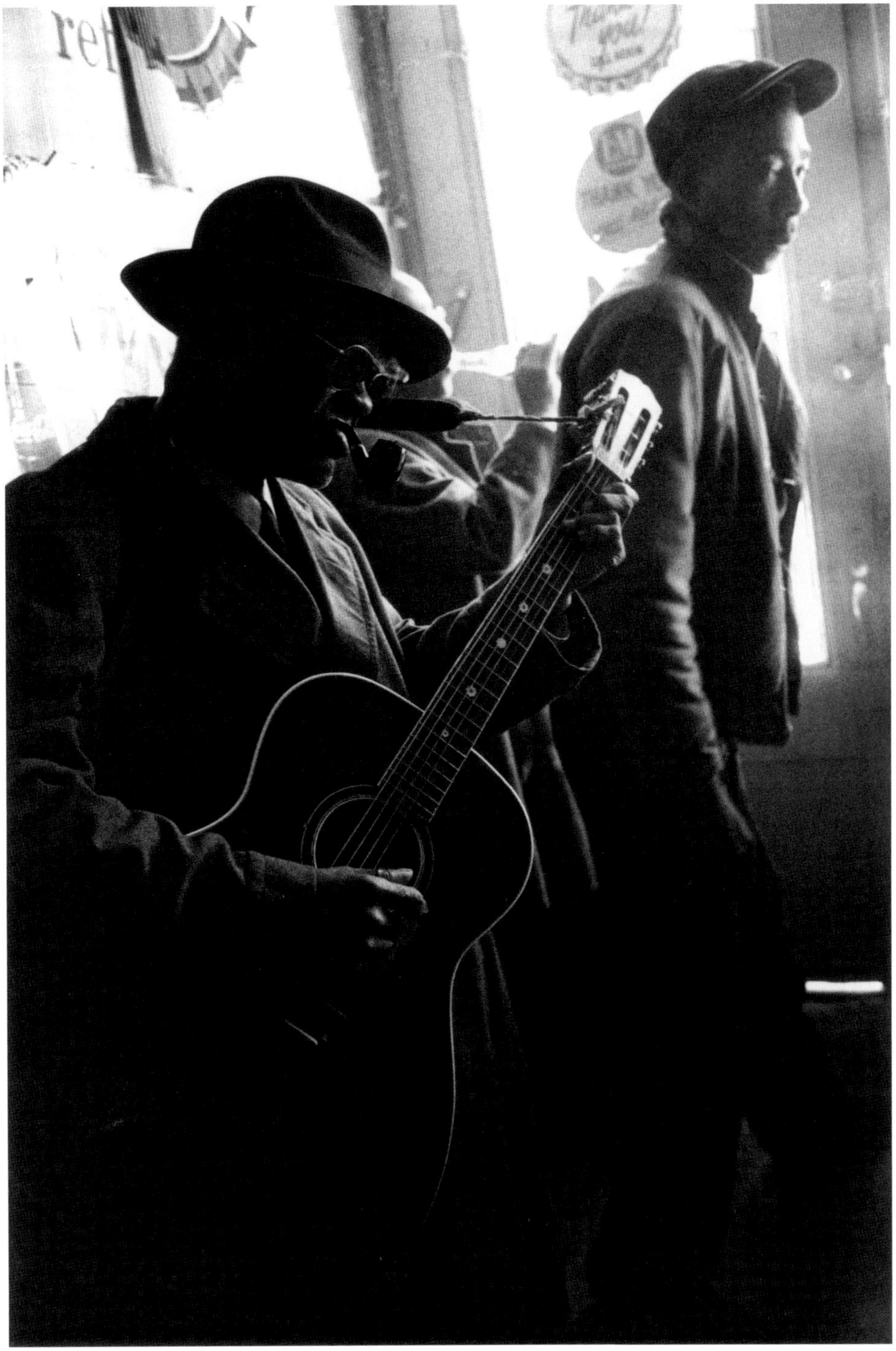

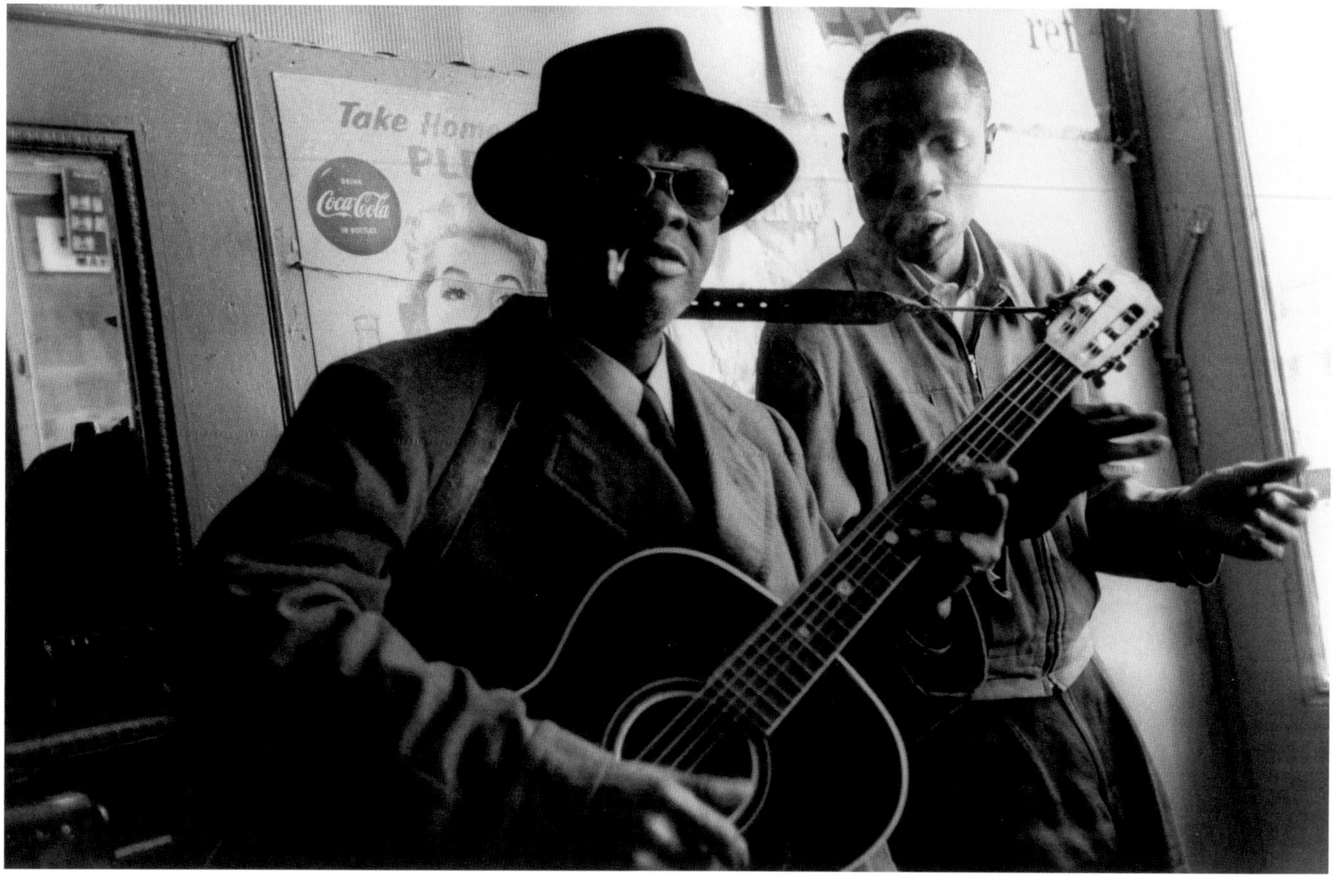
Take
Coca-Cola

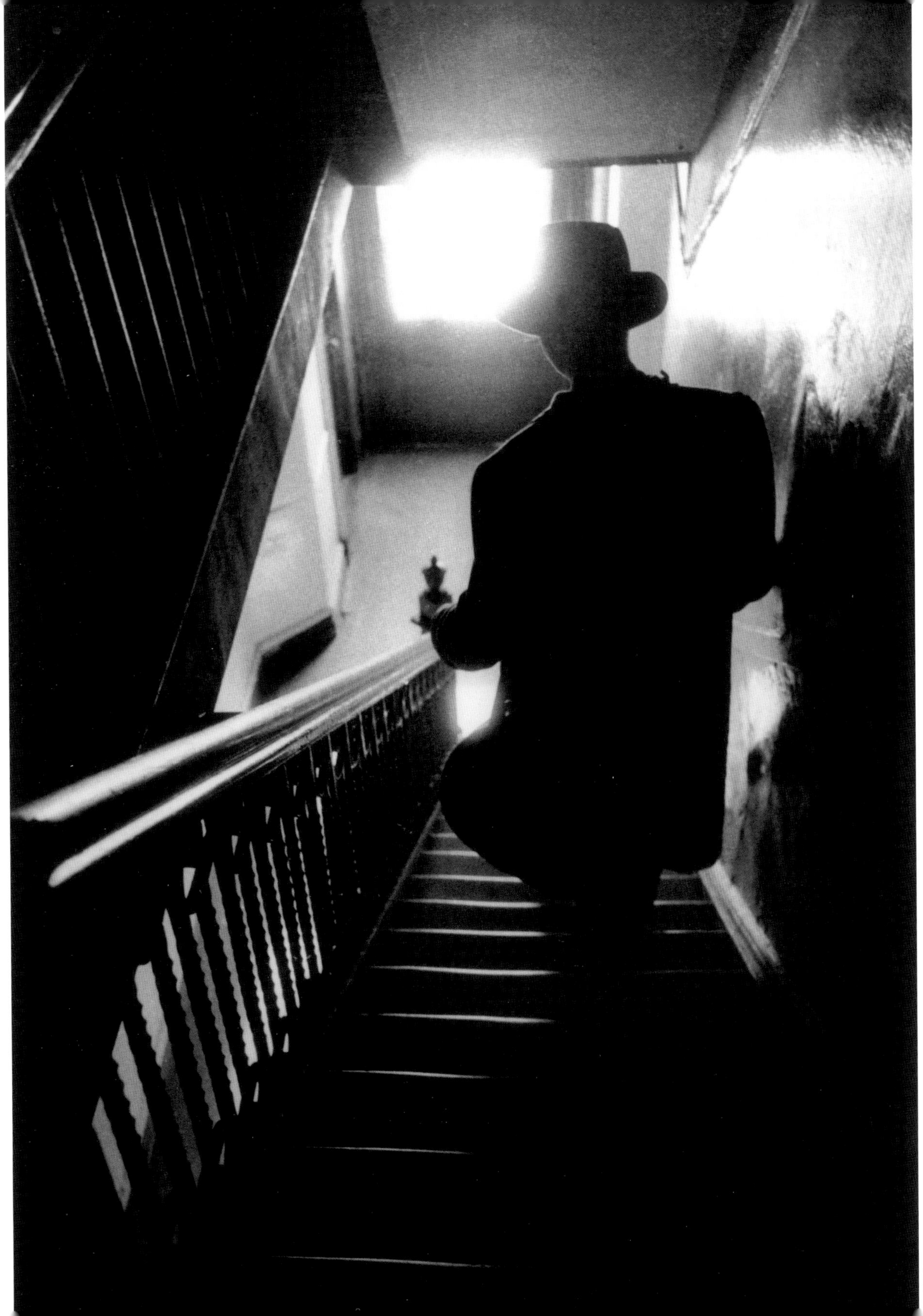

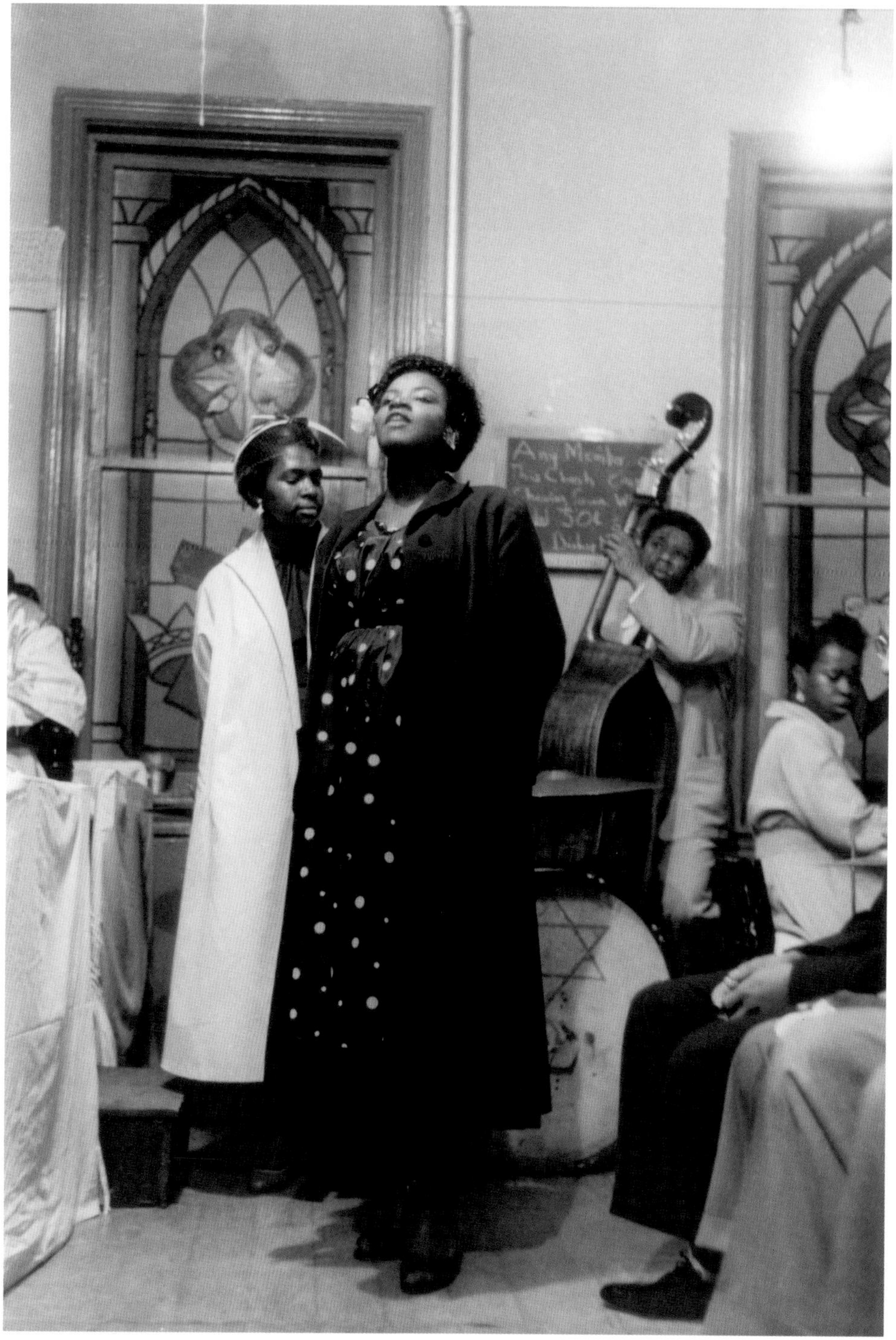

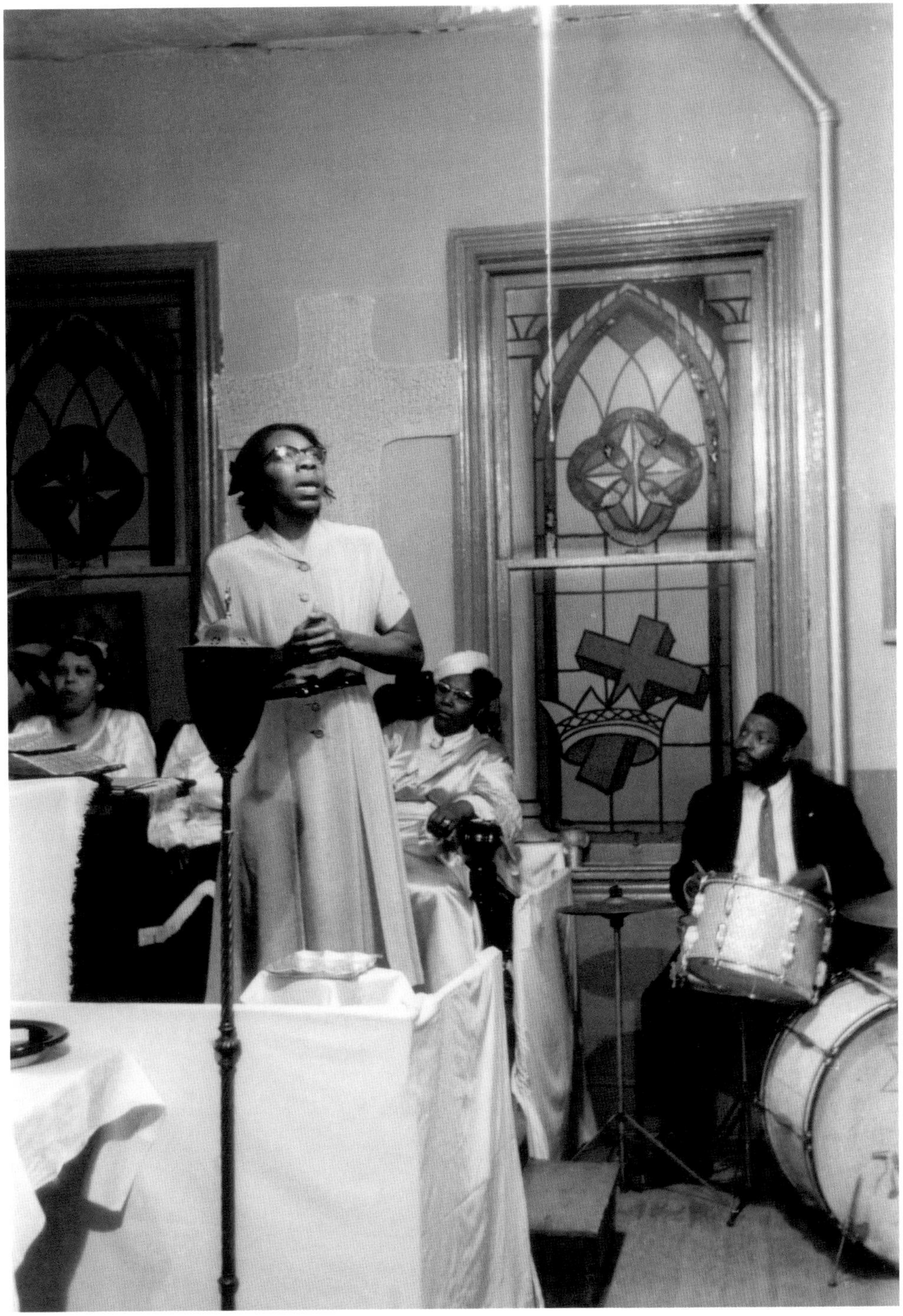

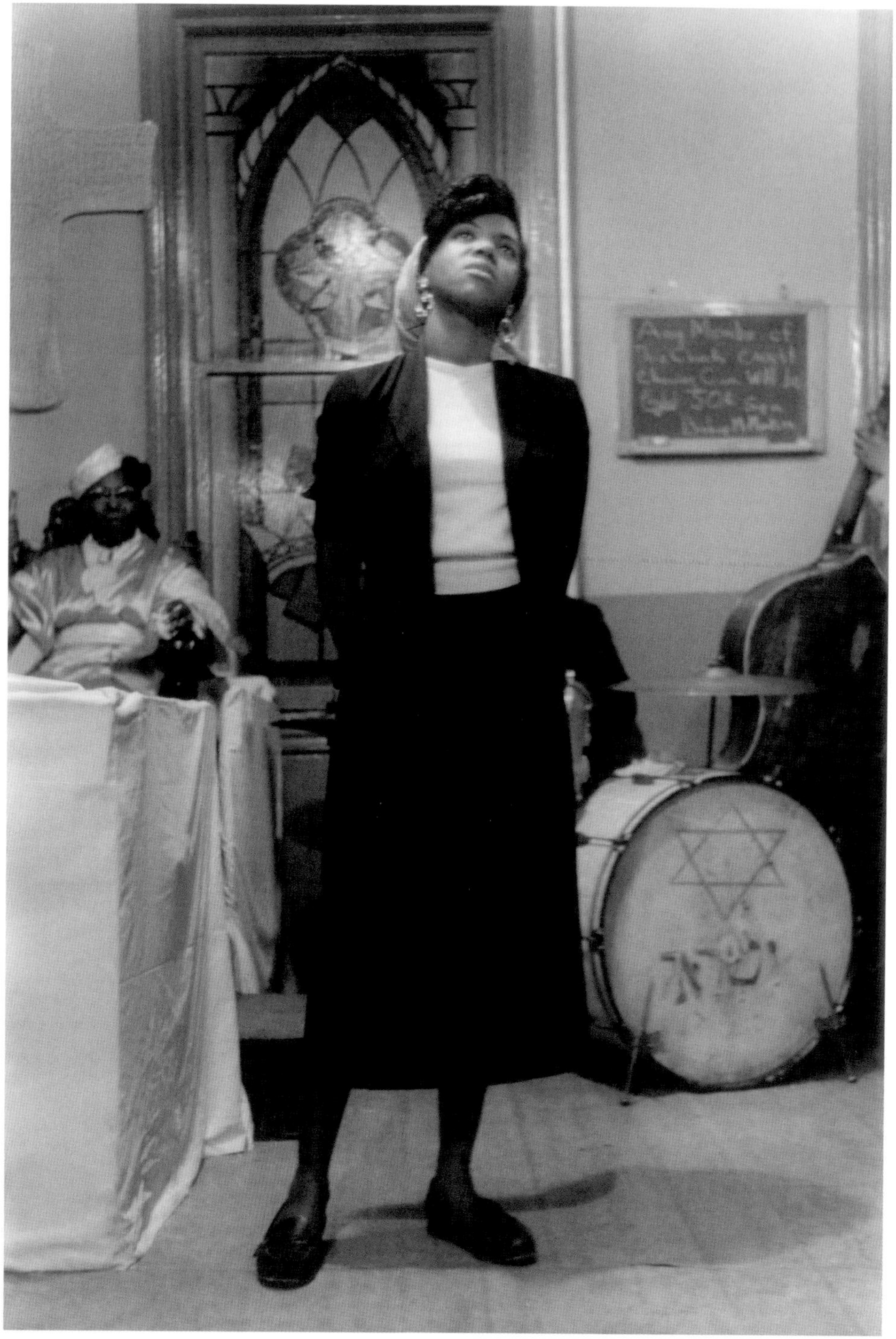

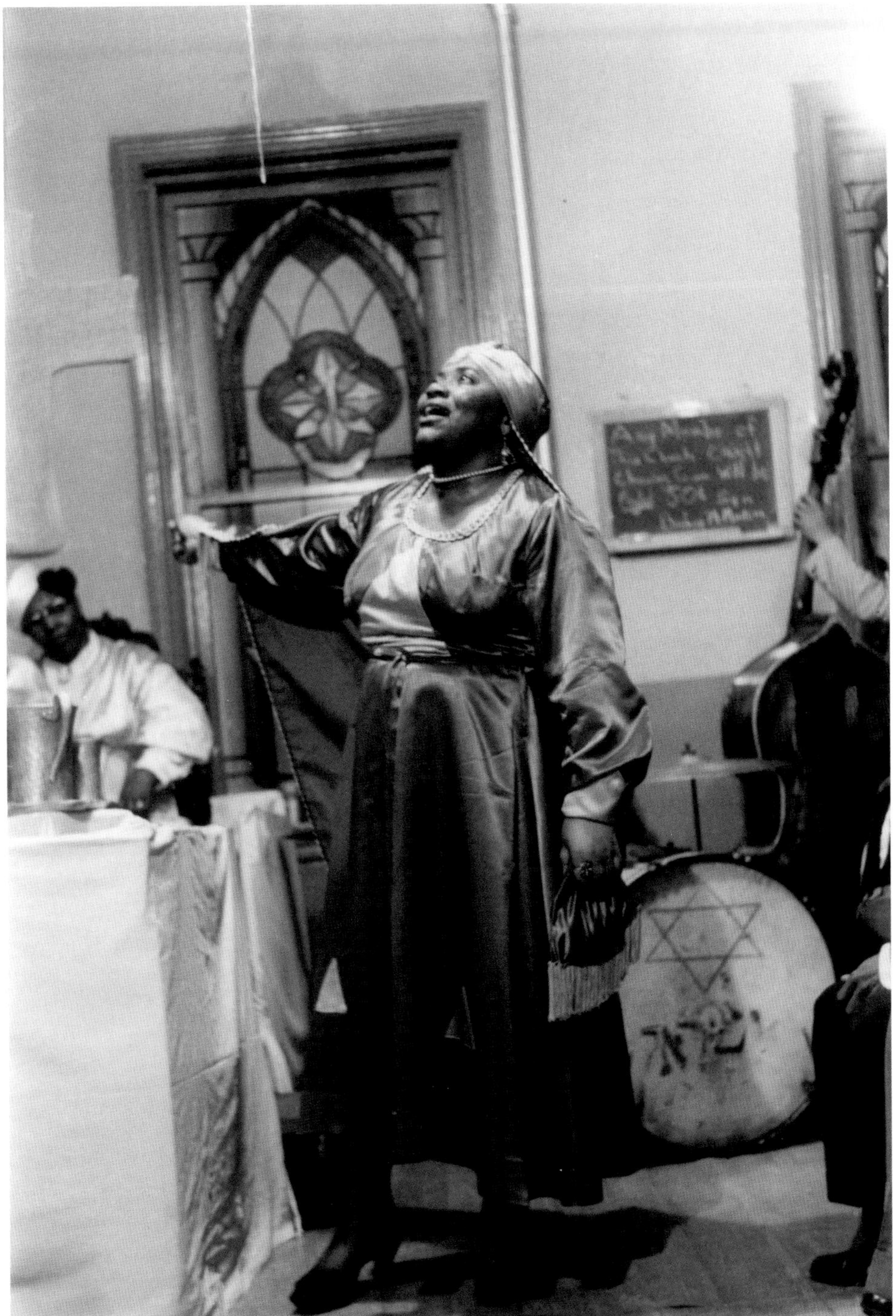

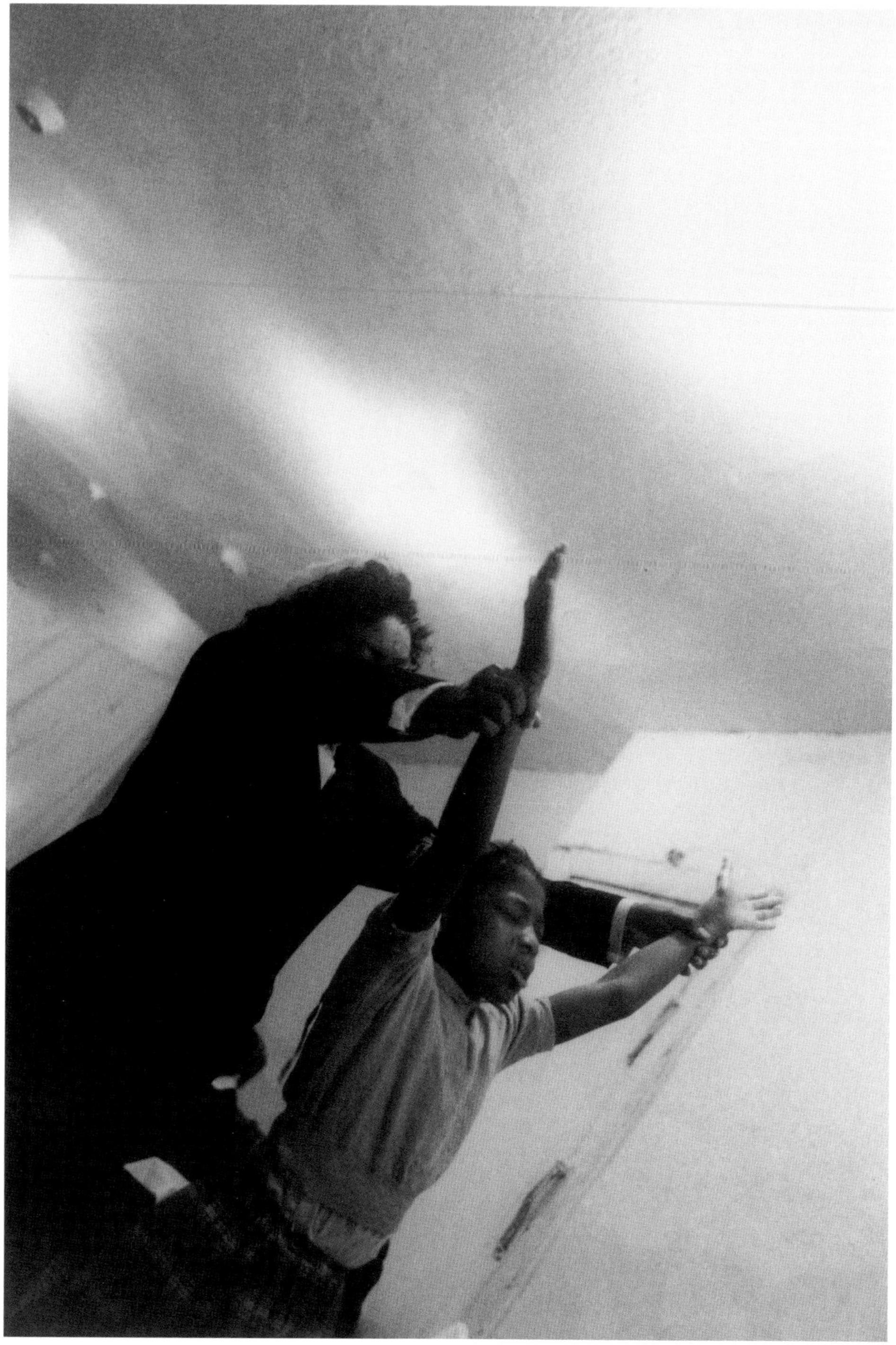

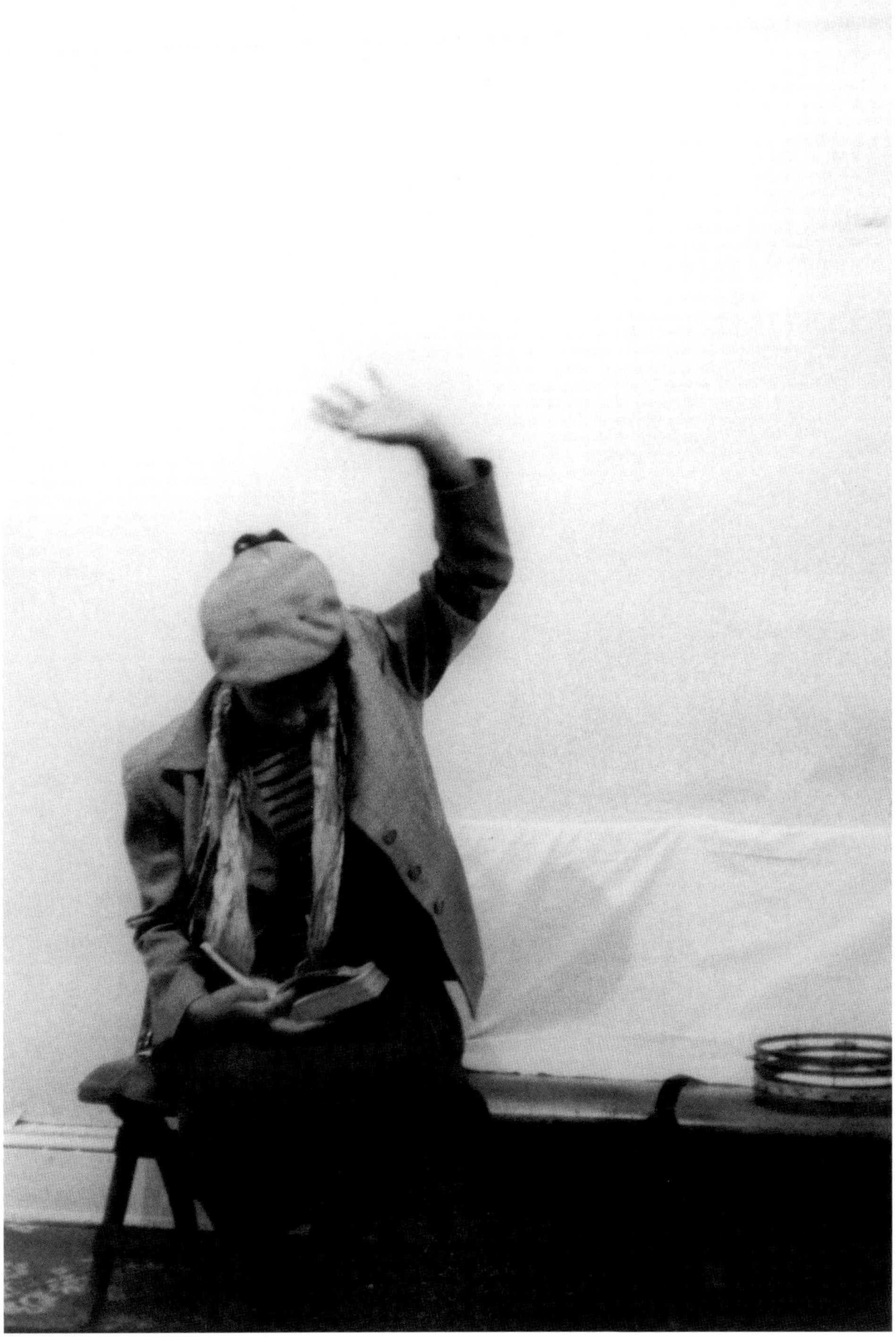

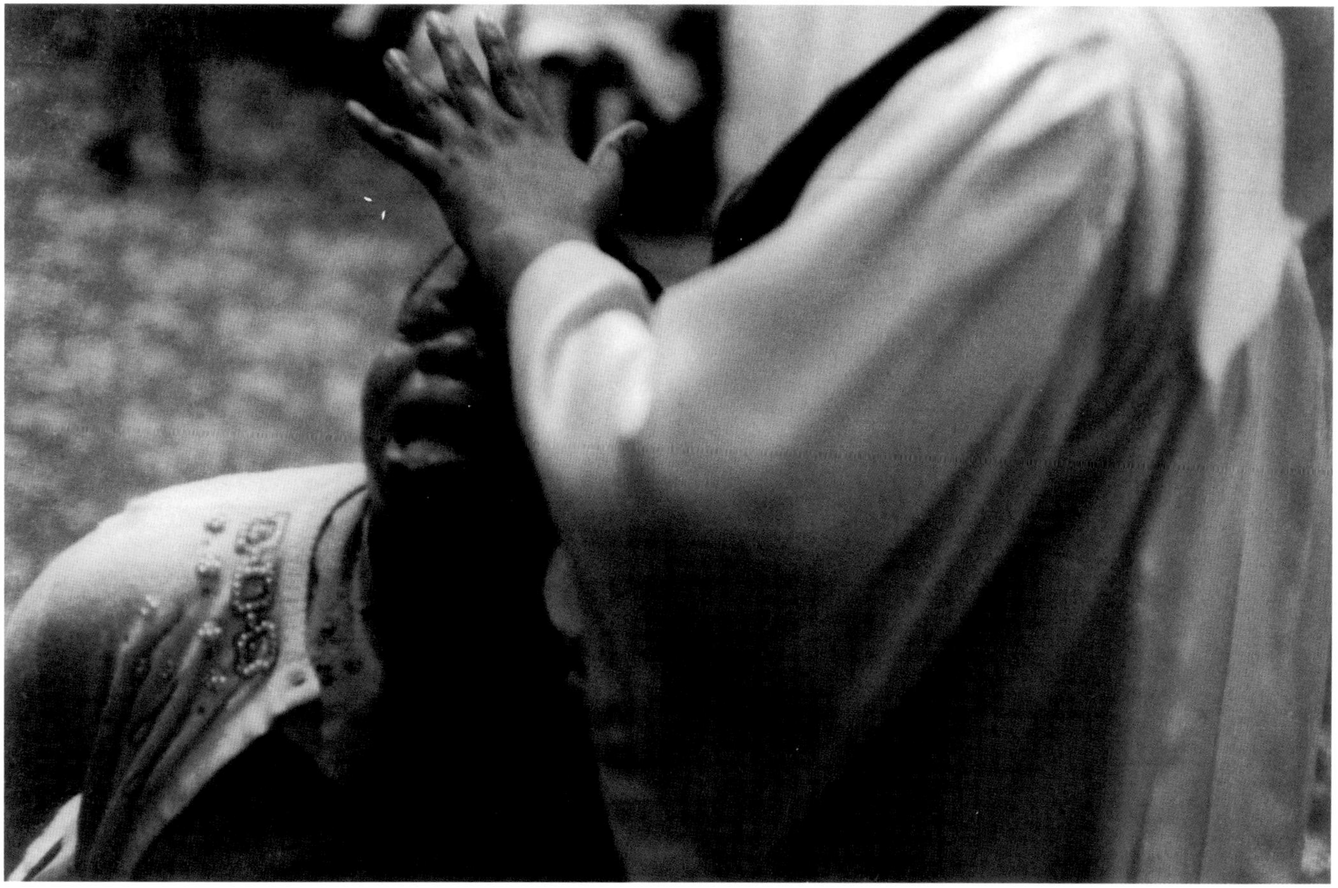

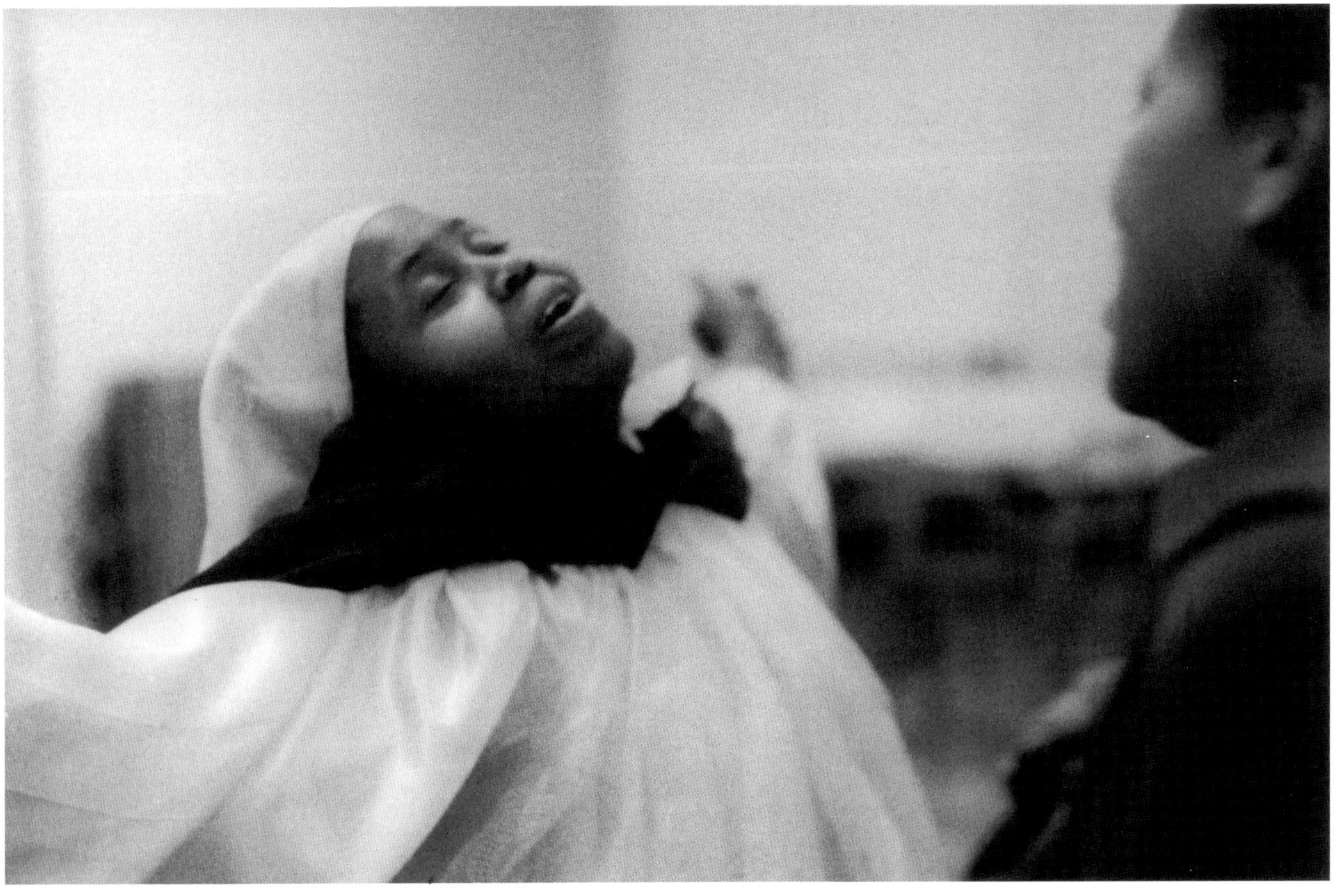

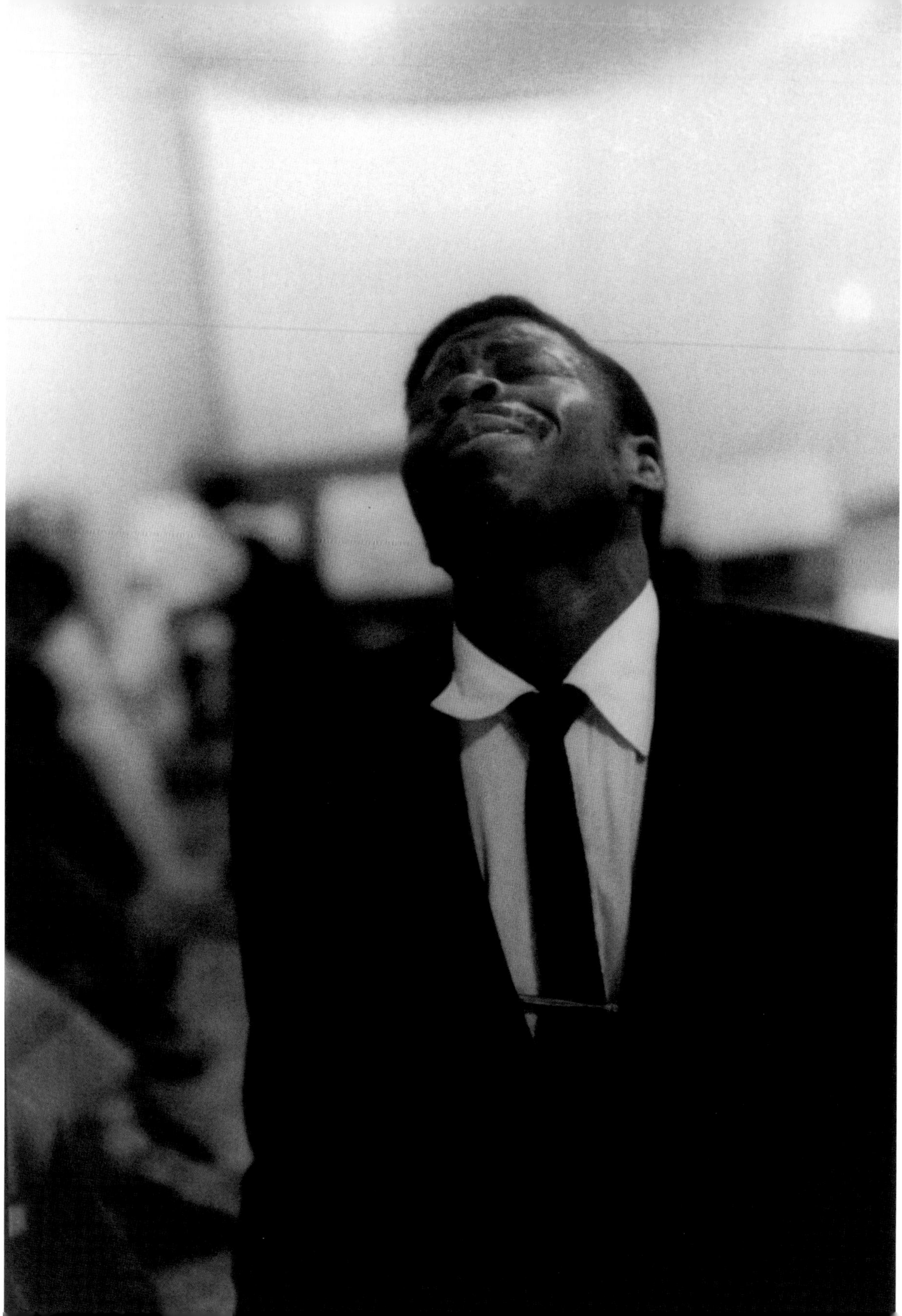

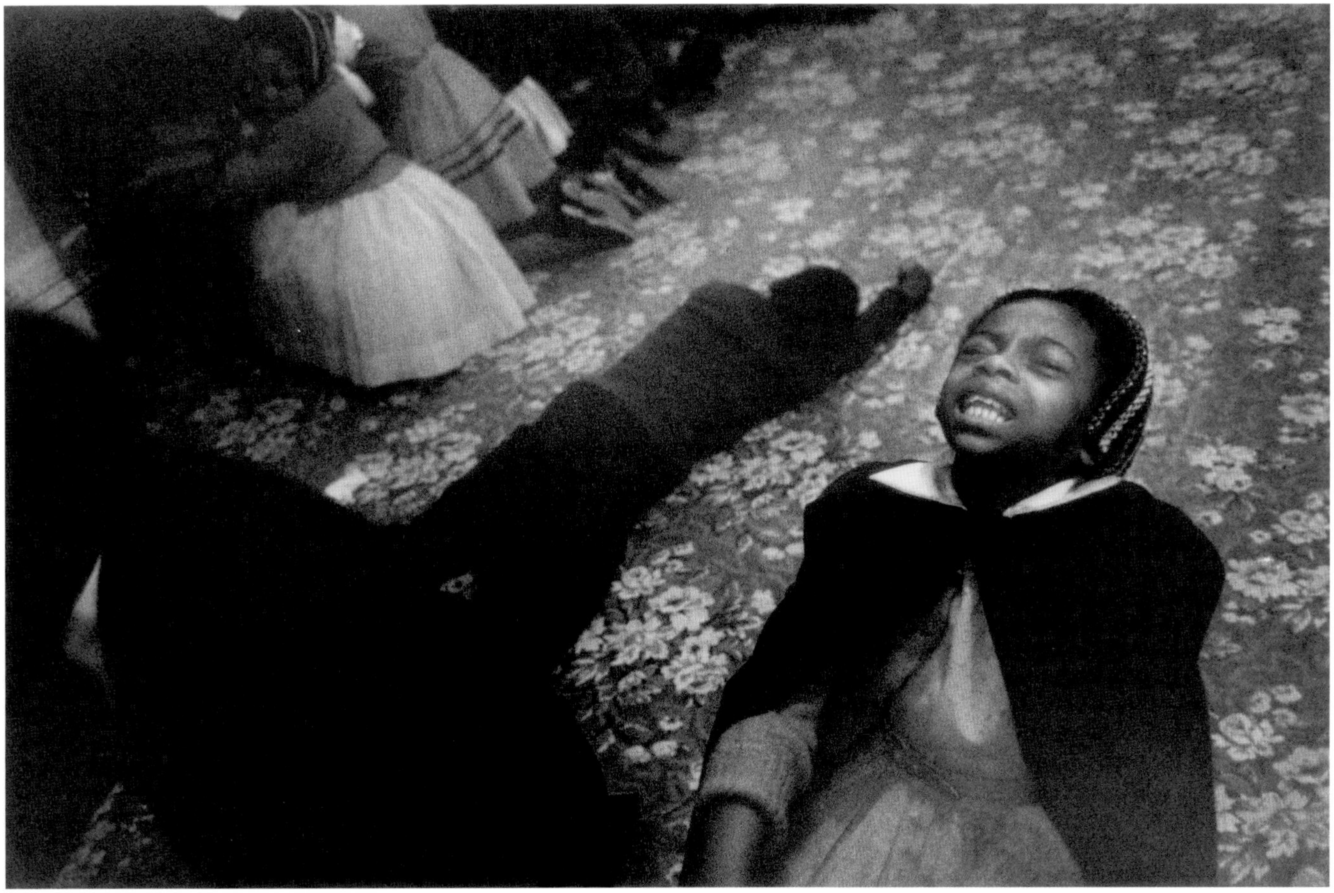

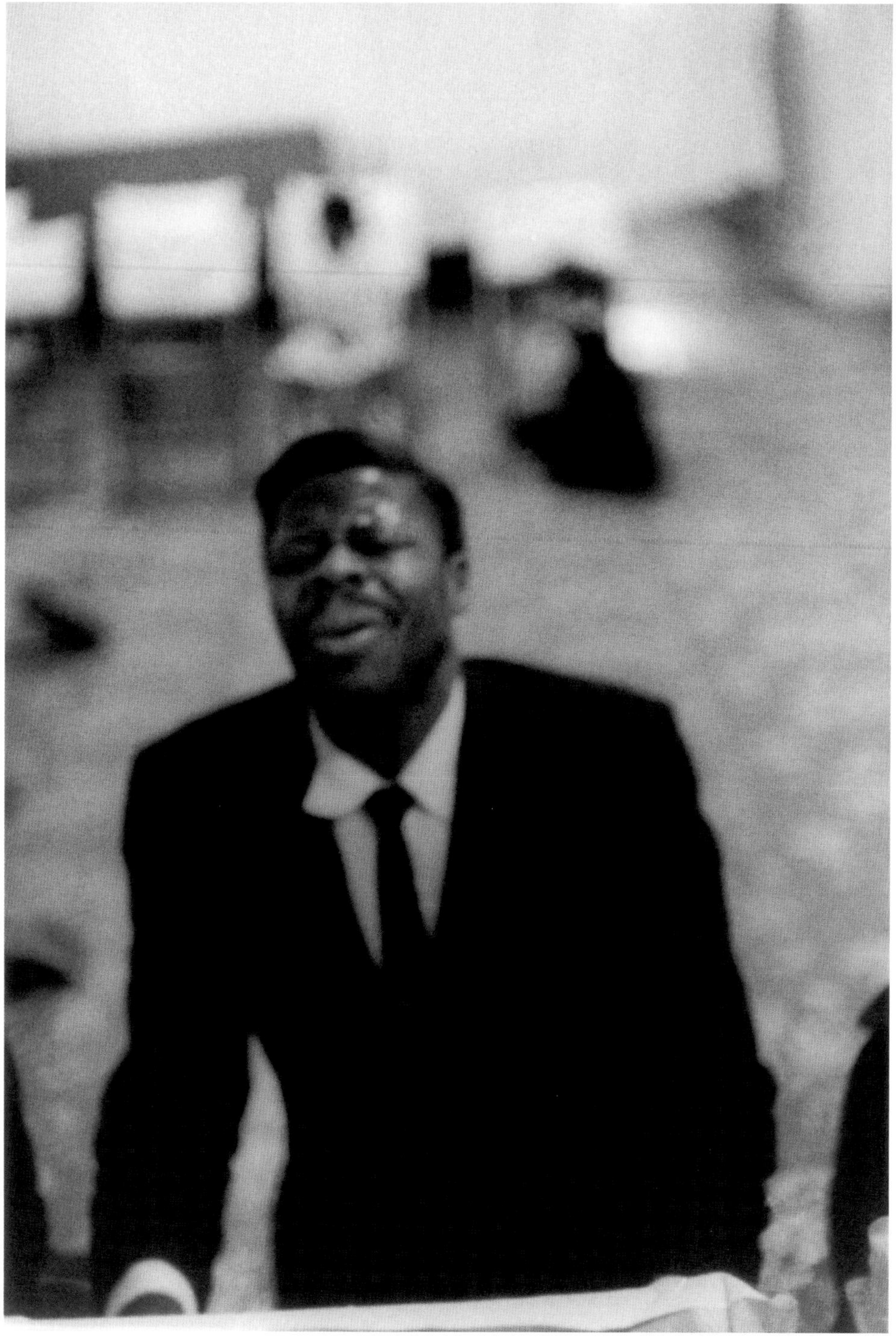

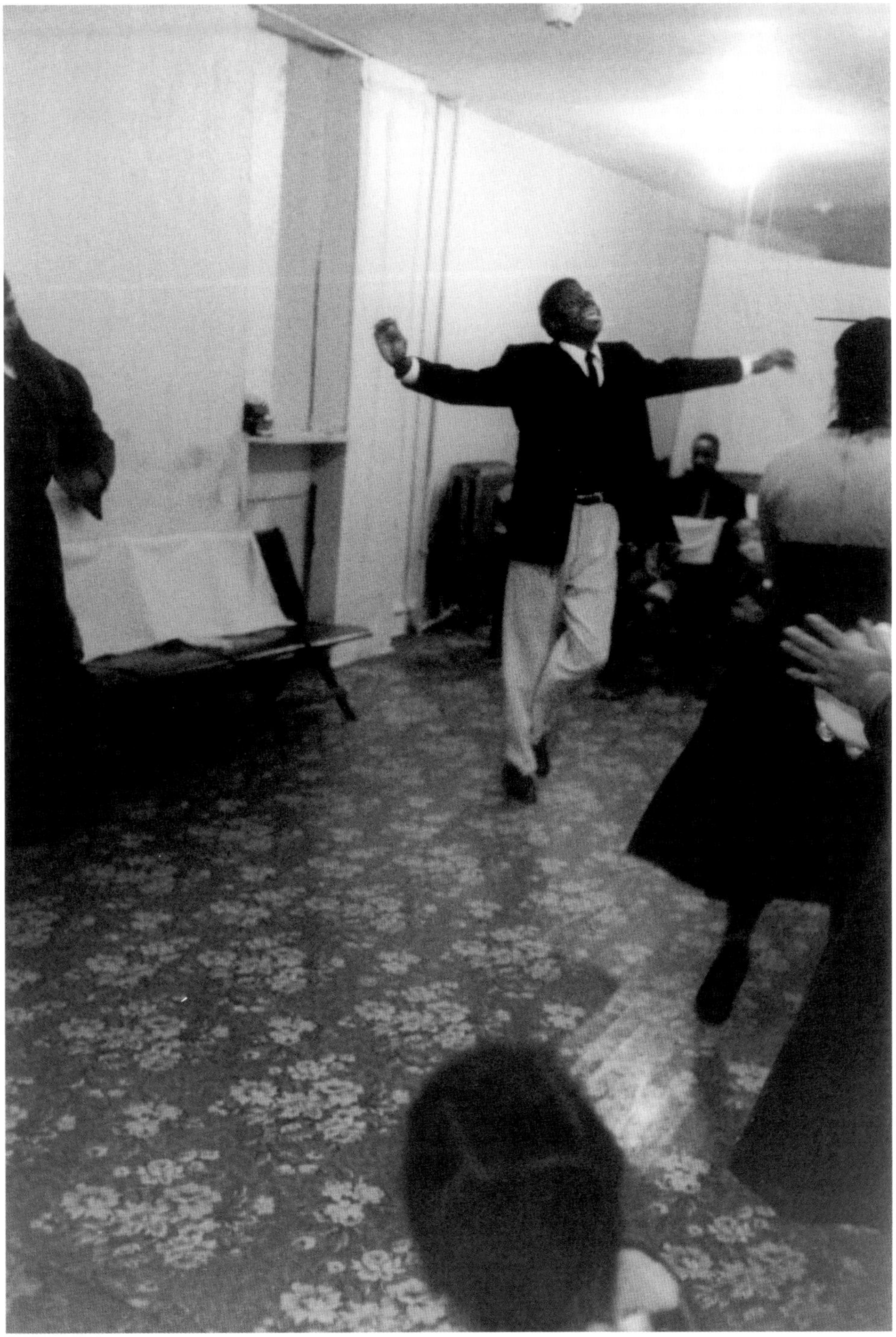

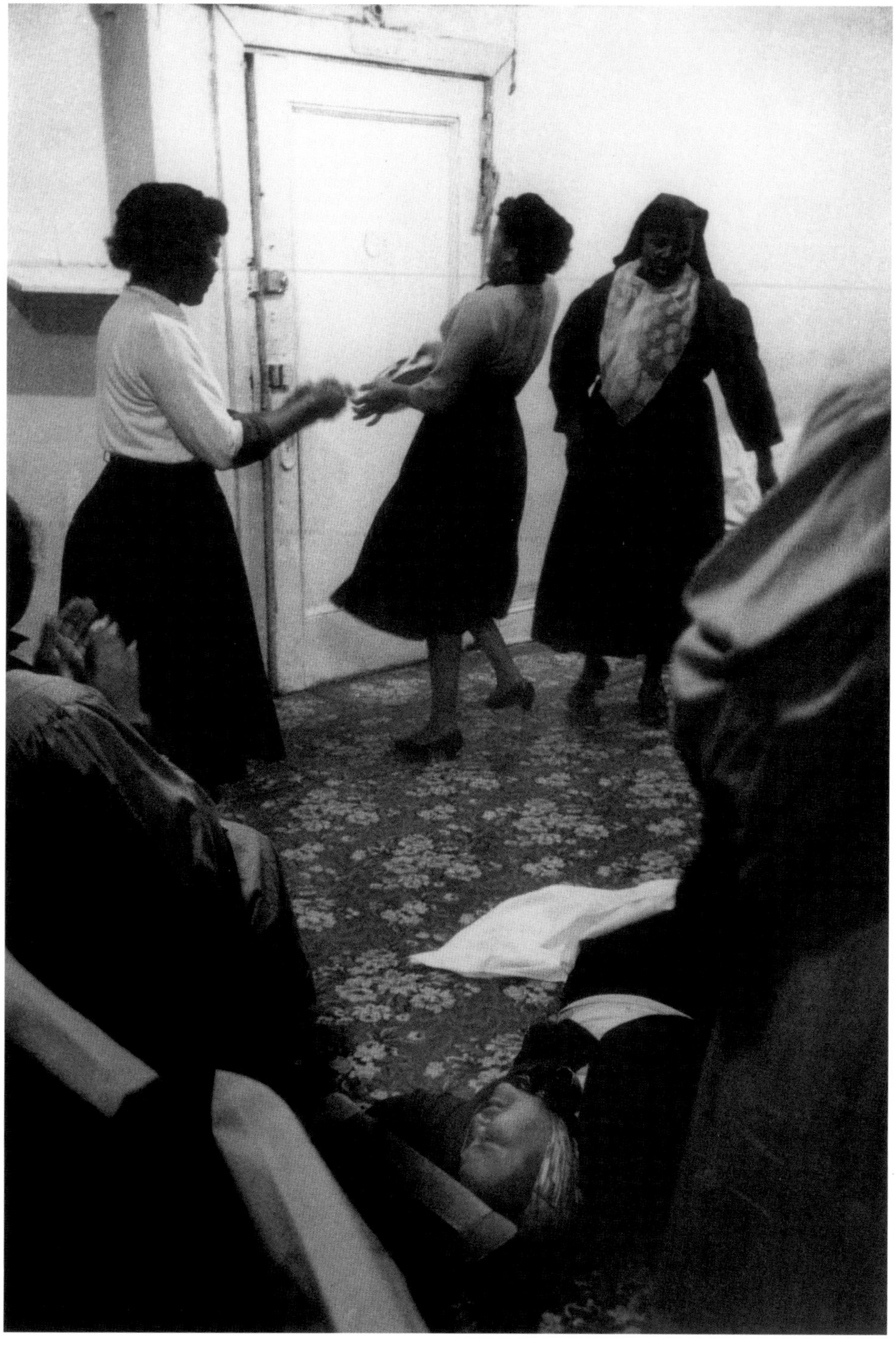

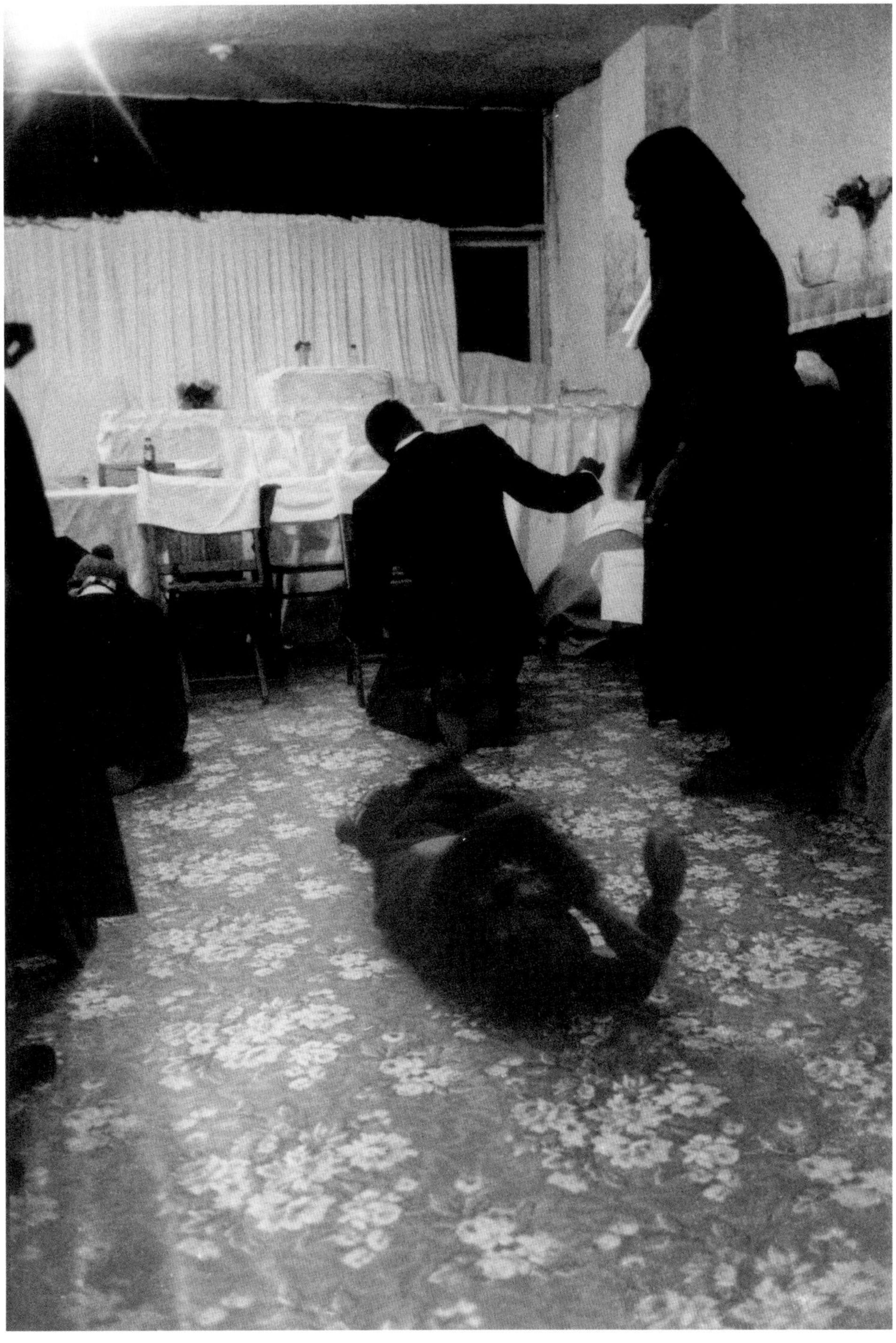

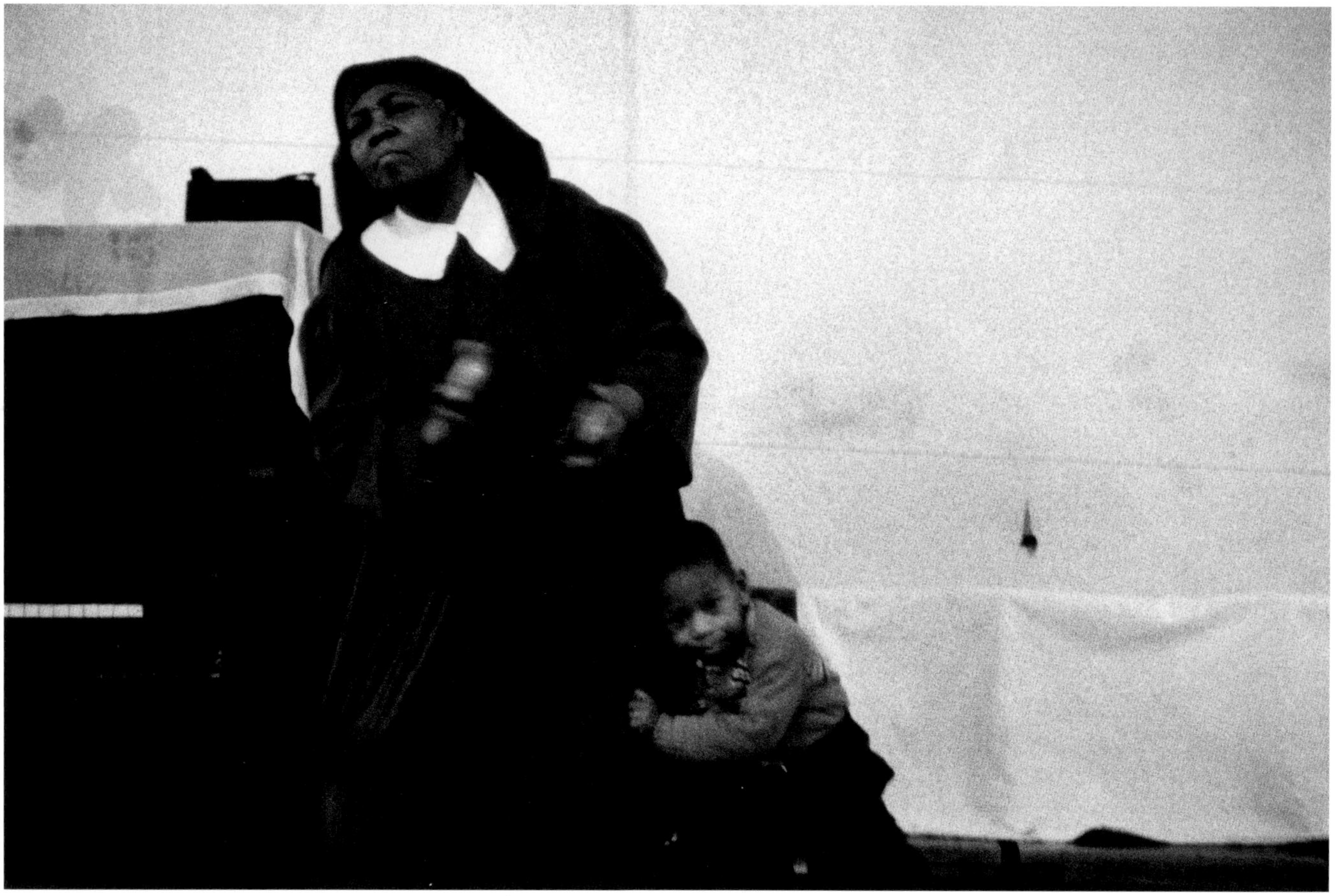

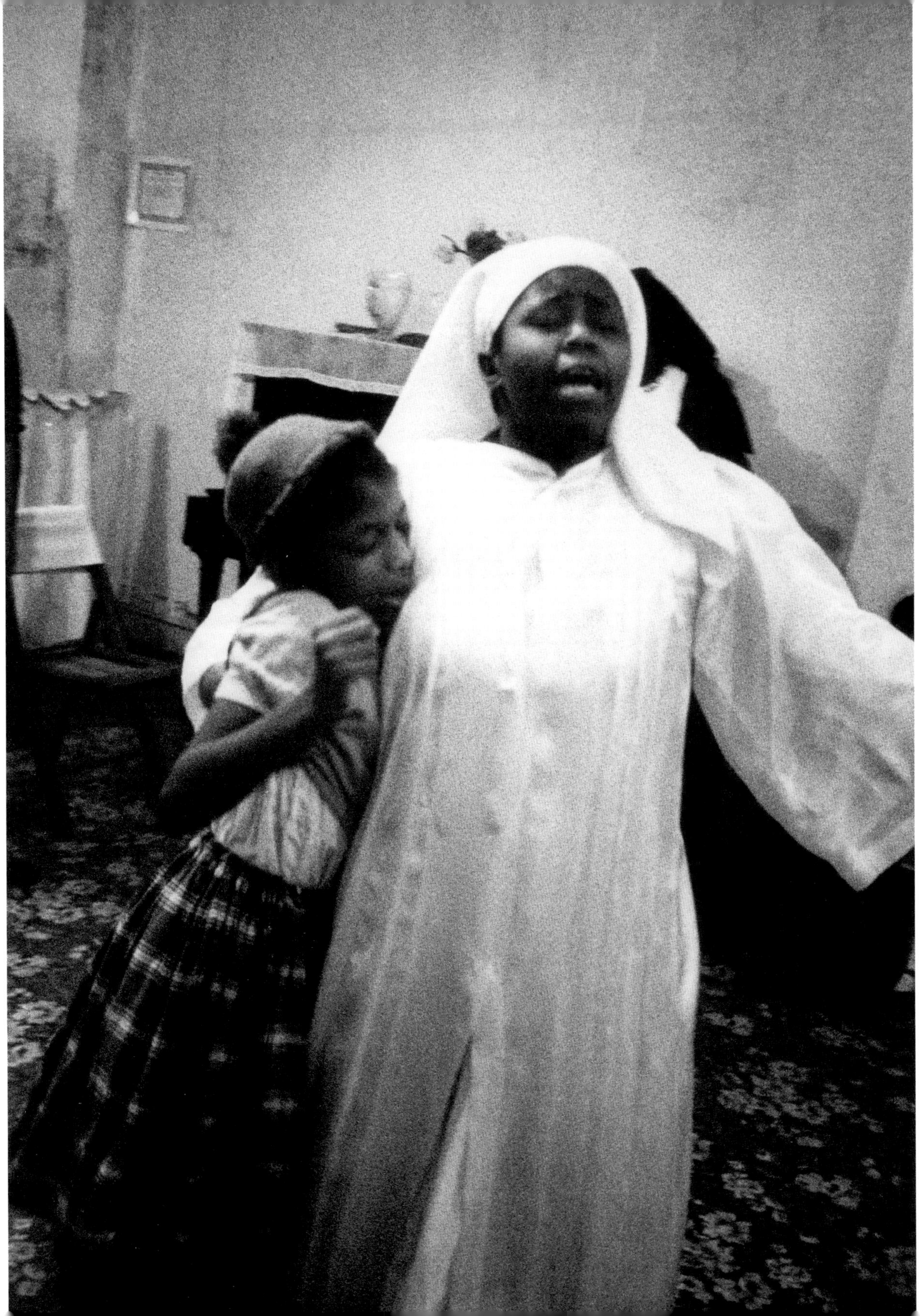

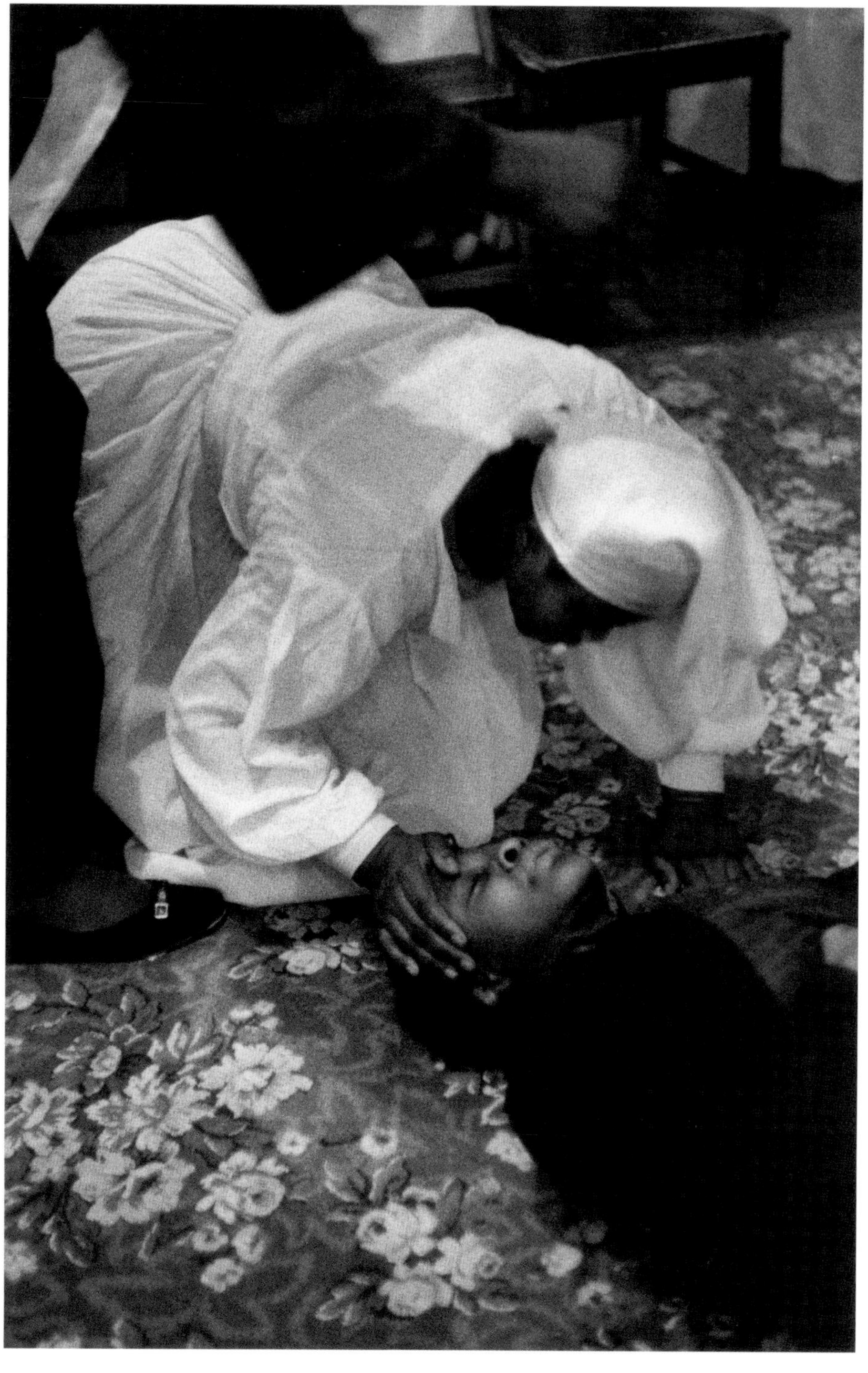

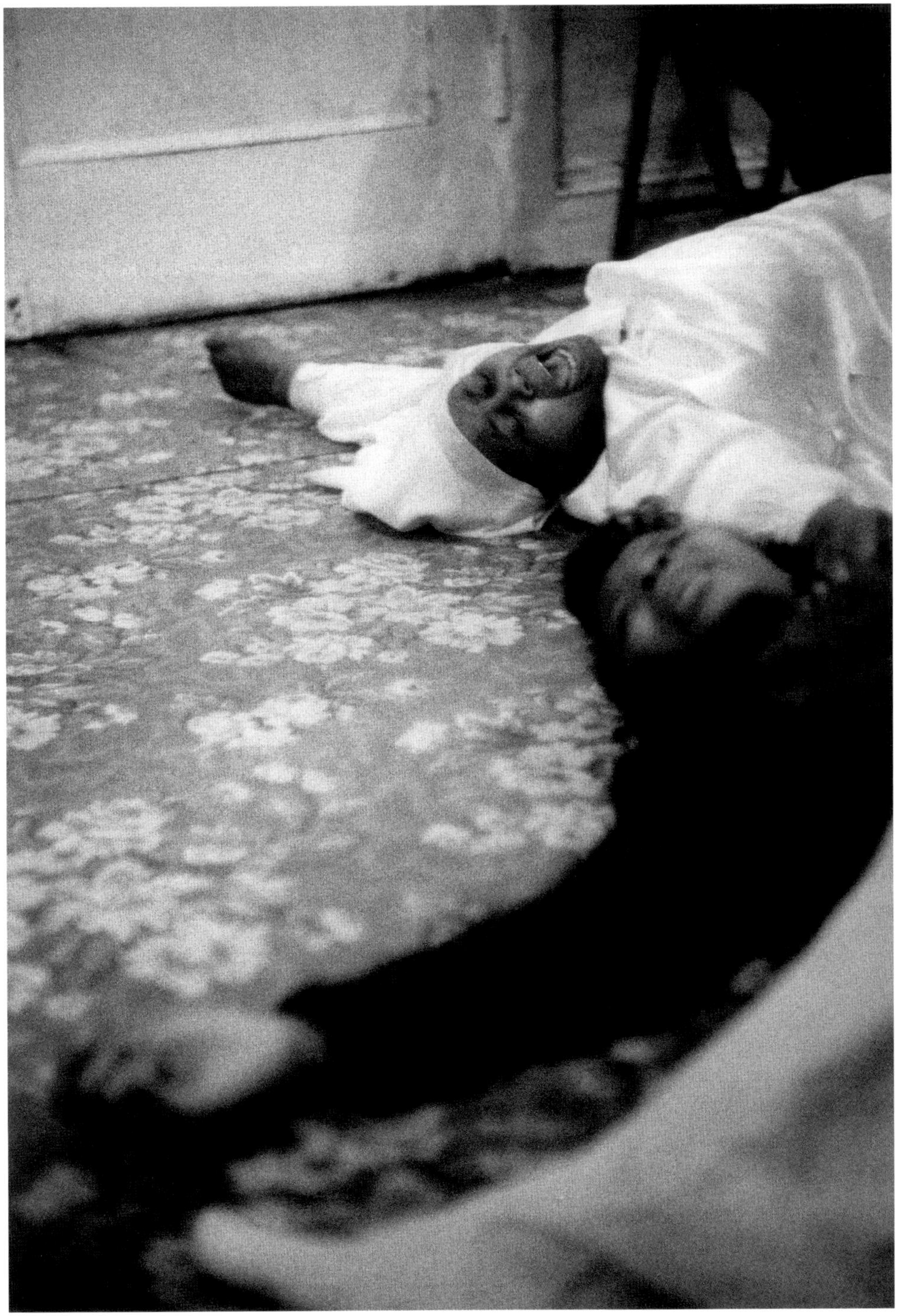

..........the voices rose again, and the music swept on again, like fire, or flood, or judgment. Then the church seemed to swell with the Power it held..........

..........someone would cry again, and the voices would begin again; there would be music by and by, and shouting, and the sound of the tambourines.

..........the tarry service moved from its first stage of steady murmuring, broken by moans and now and again an isolated cry, into that stage of tears and groaning, of calling aloud and singing, which was like the labor of a woman about to be delivered of her child.

On this threshing-floor the child was the soul that struggled to the light, and it was the church that was in labor, that did not cease to push and pull, calling on the name of Jesus.

..........the rebirth of the soul was perpetual; only rebirth every hour could stay the hand of Satan.

Excerpts from "Go Tell It on the Mountain" by James Baldwin

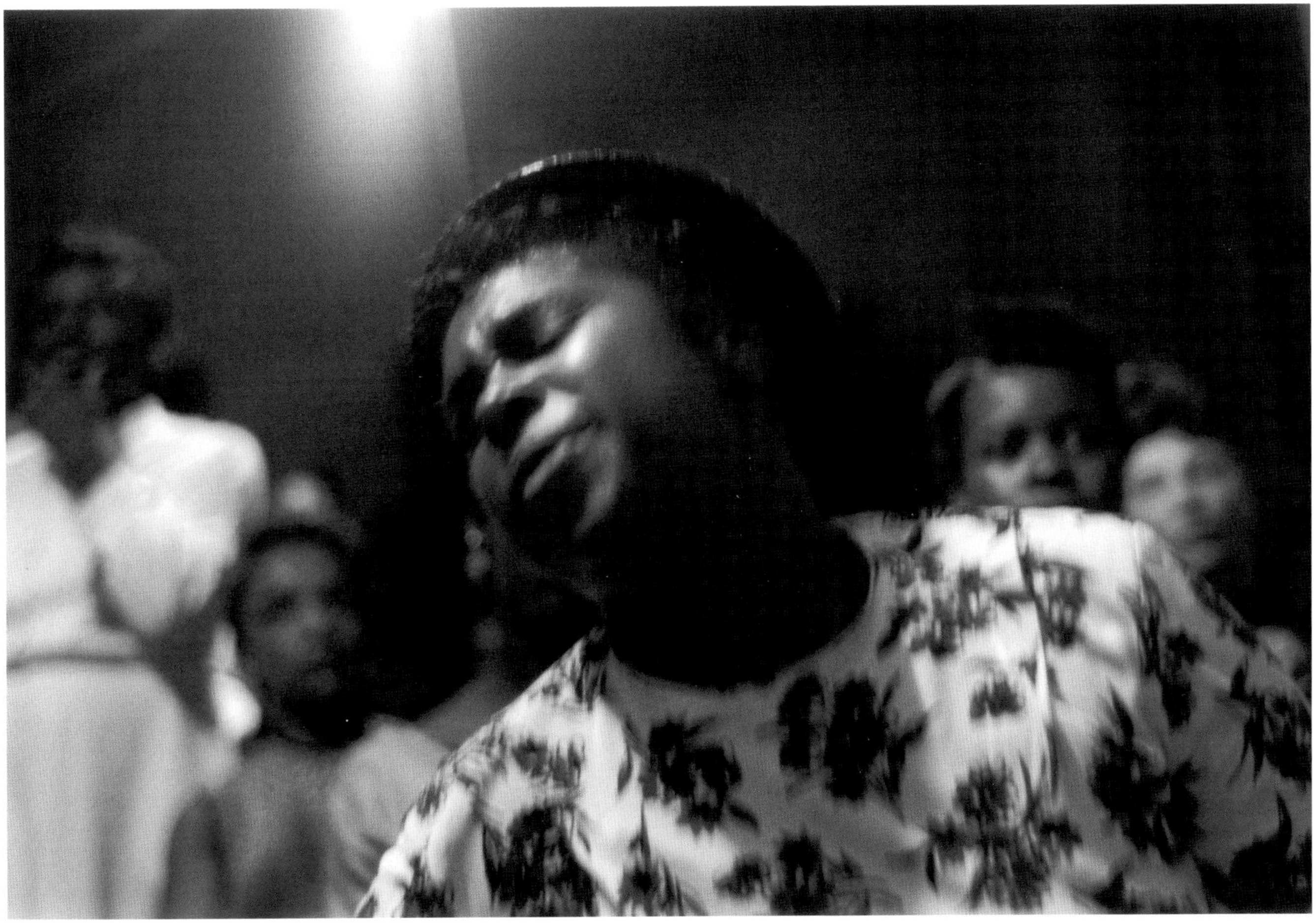

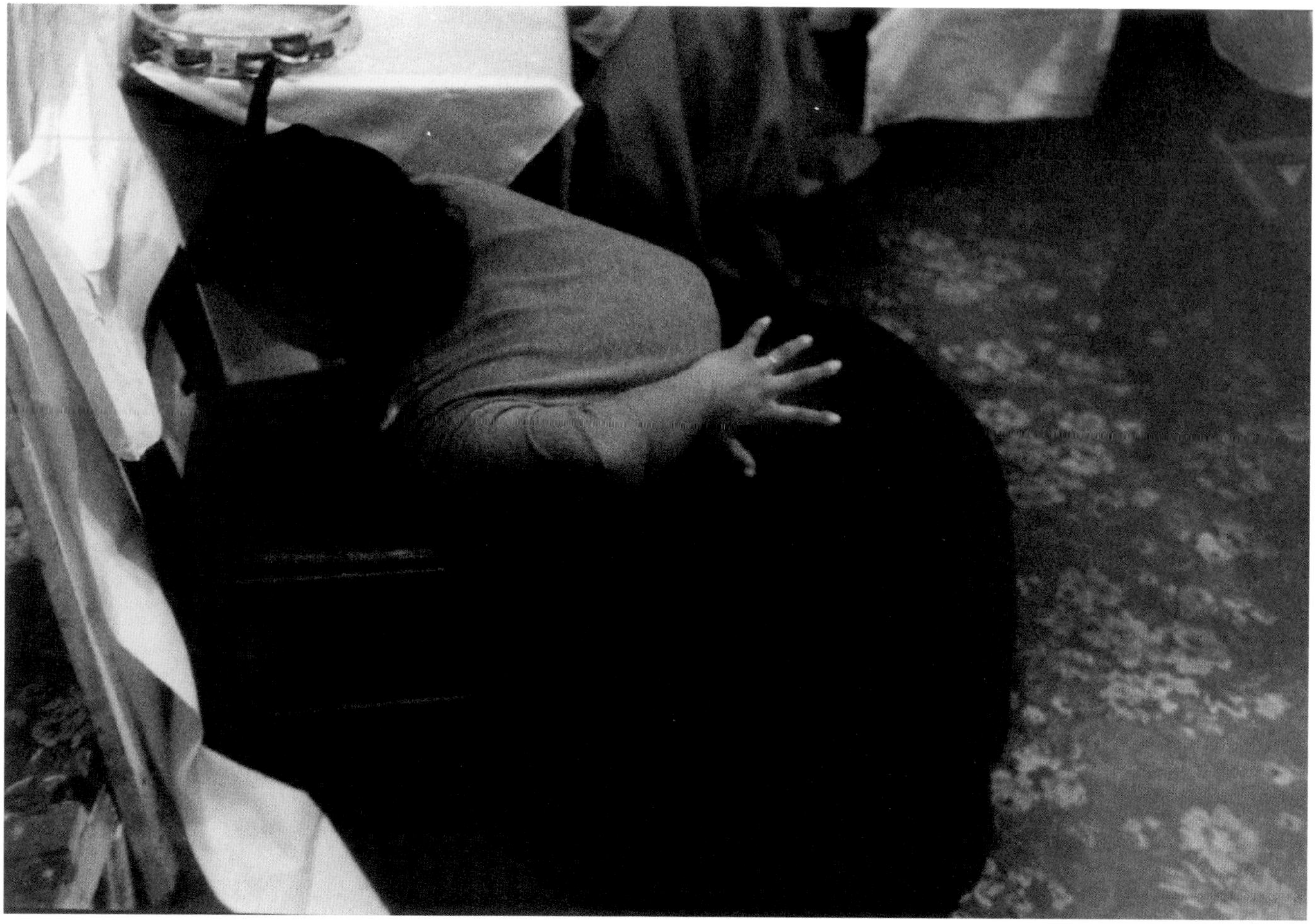

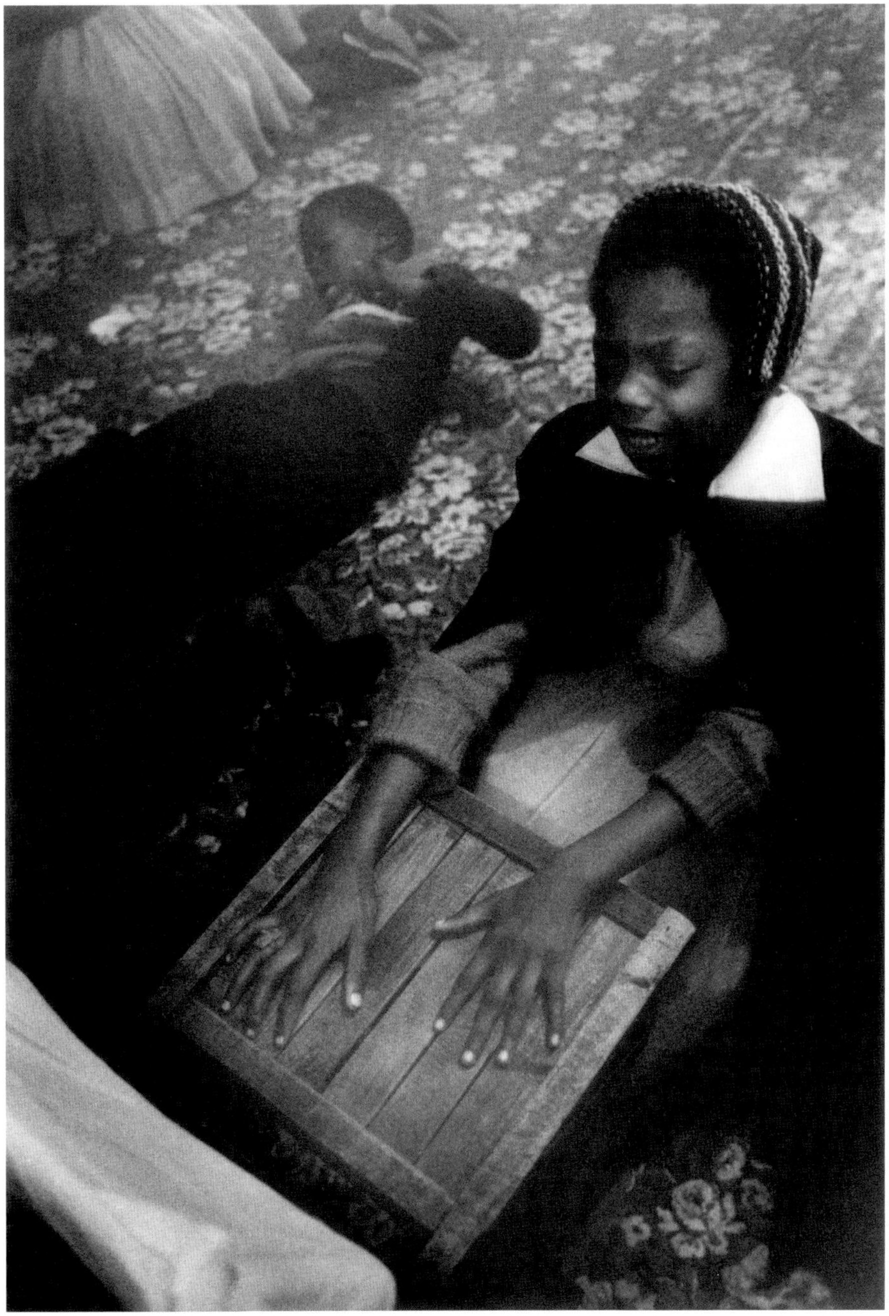

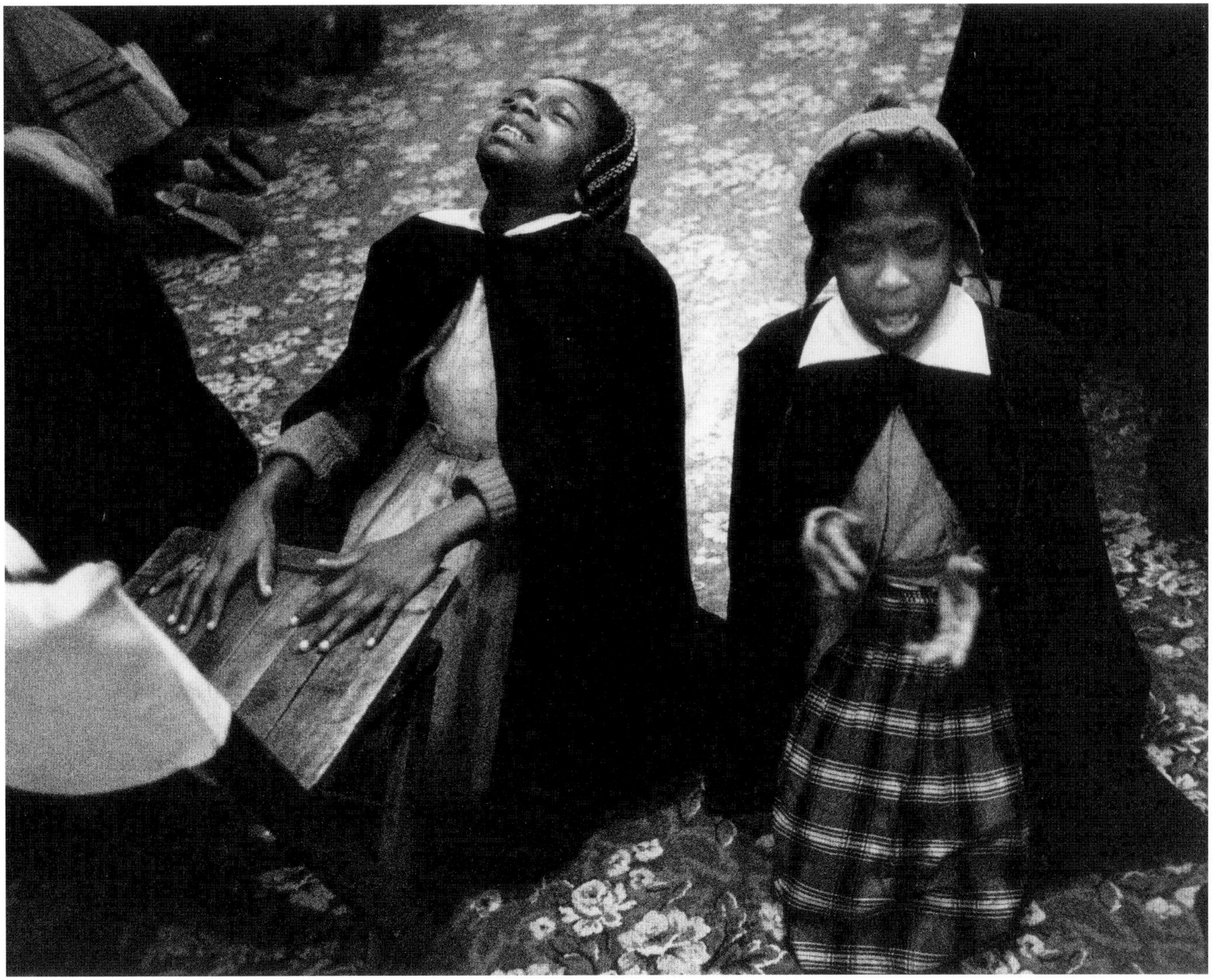

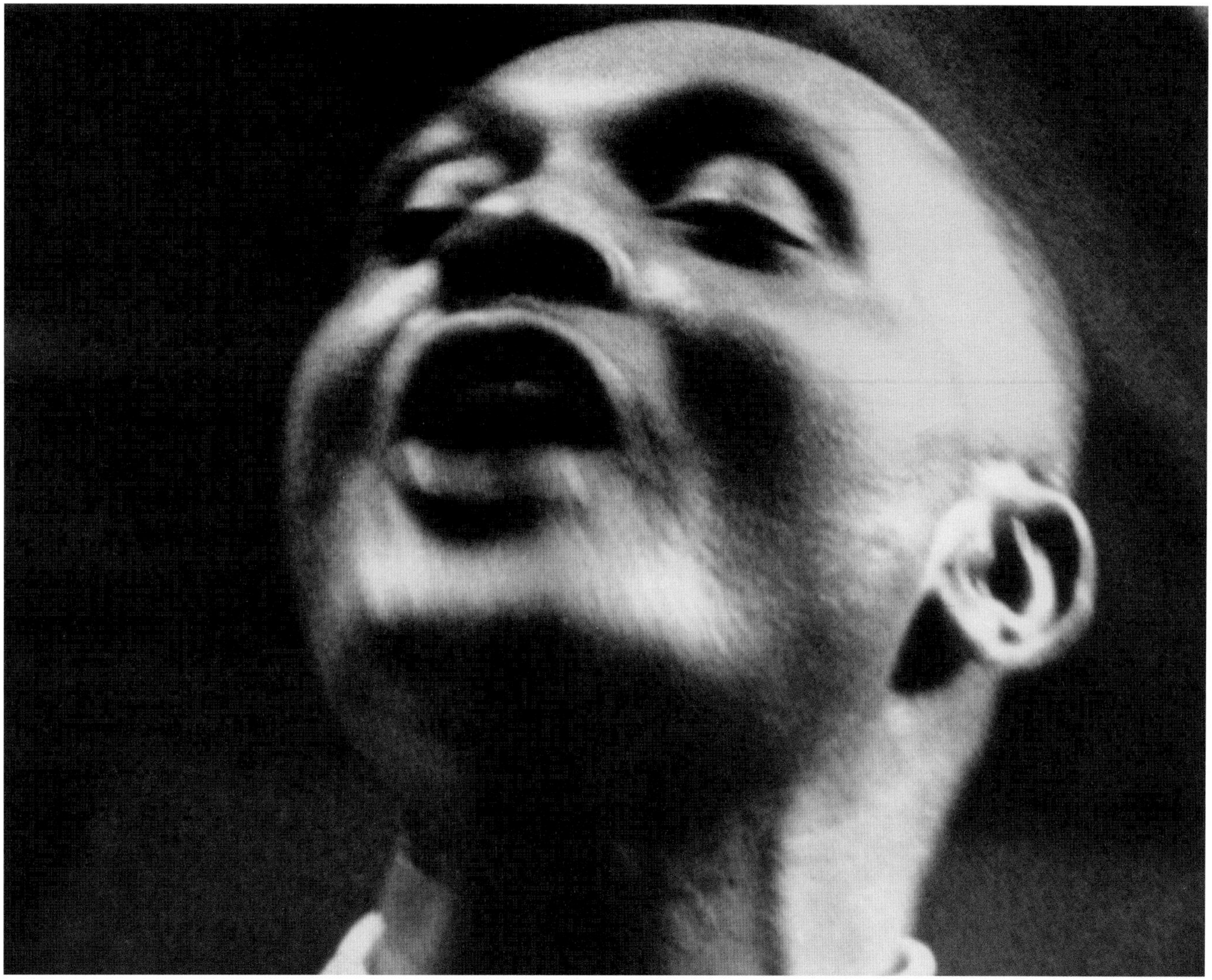

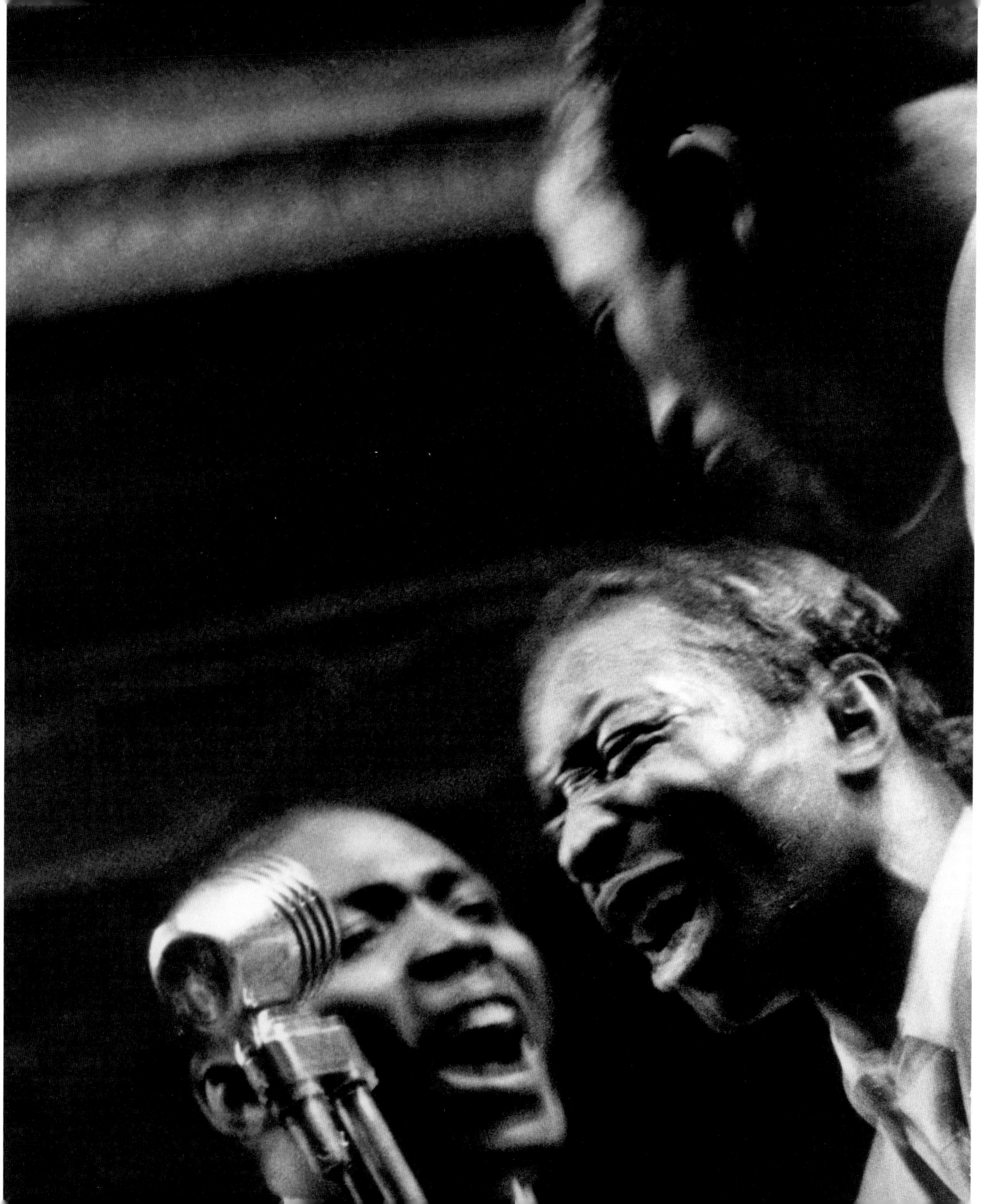

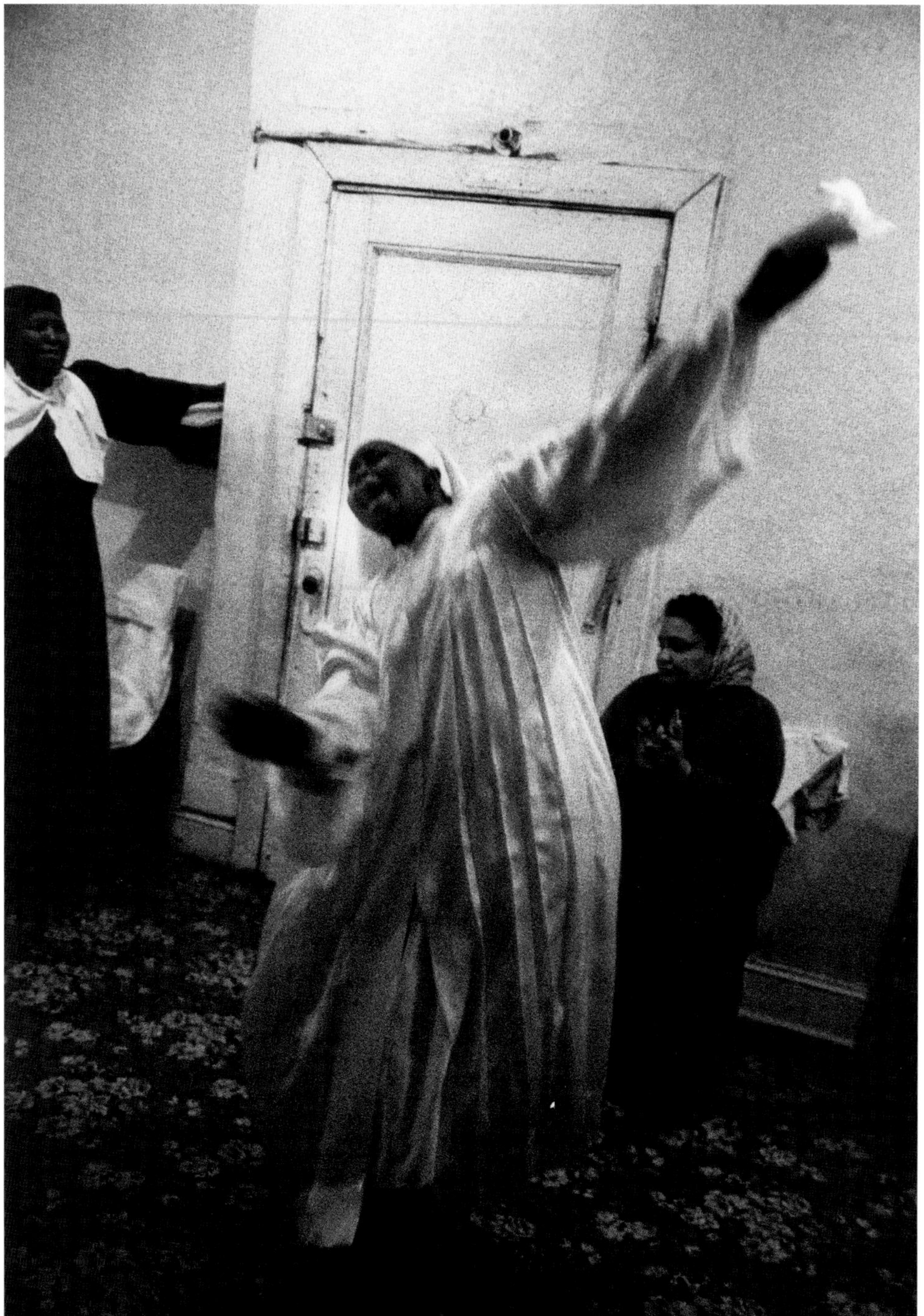

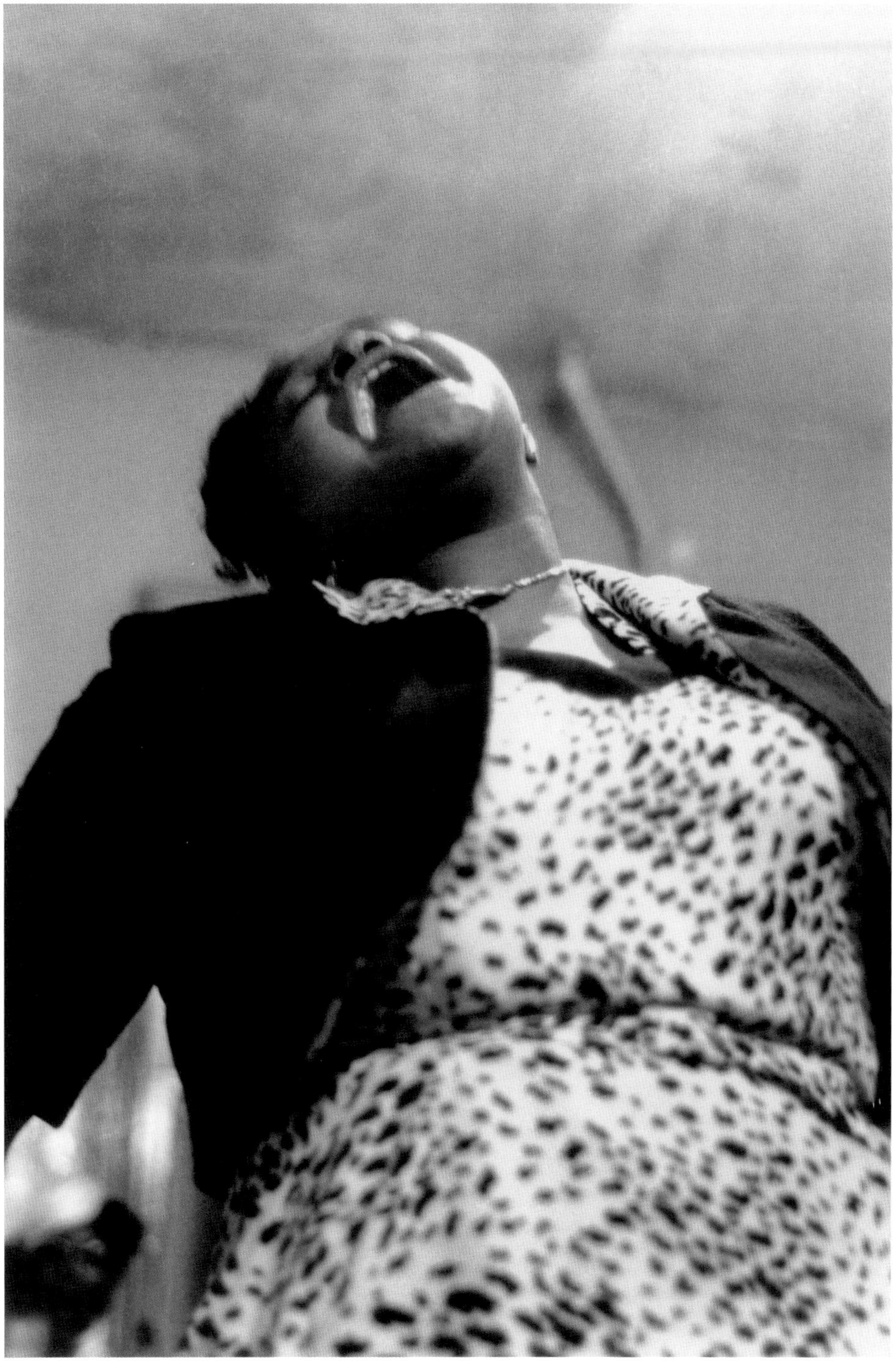

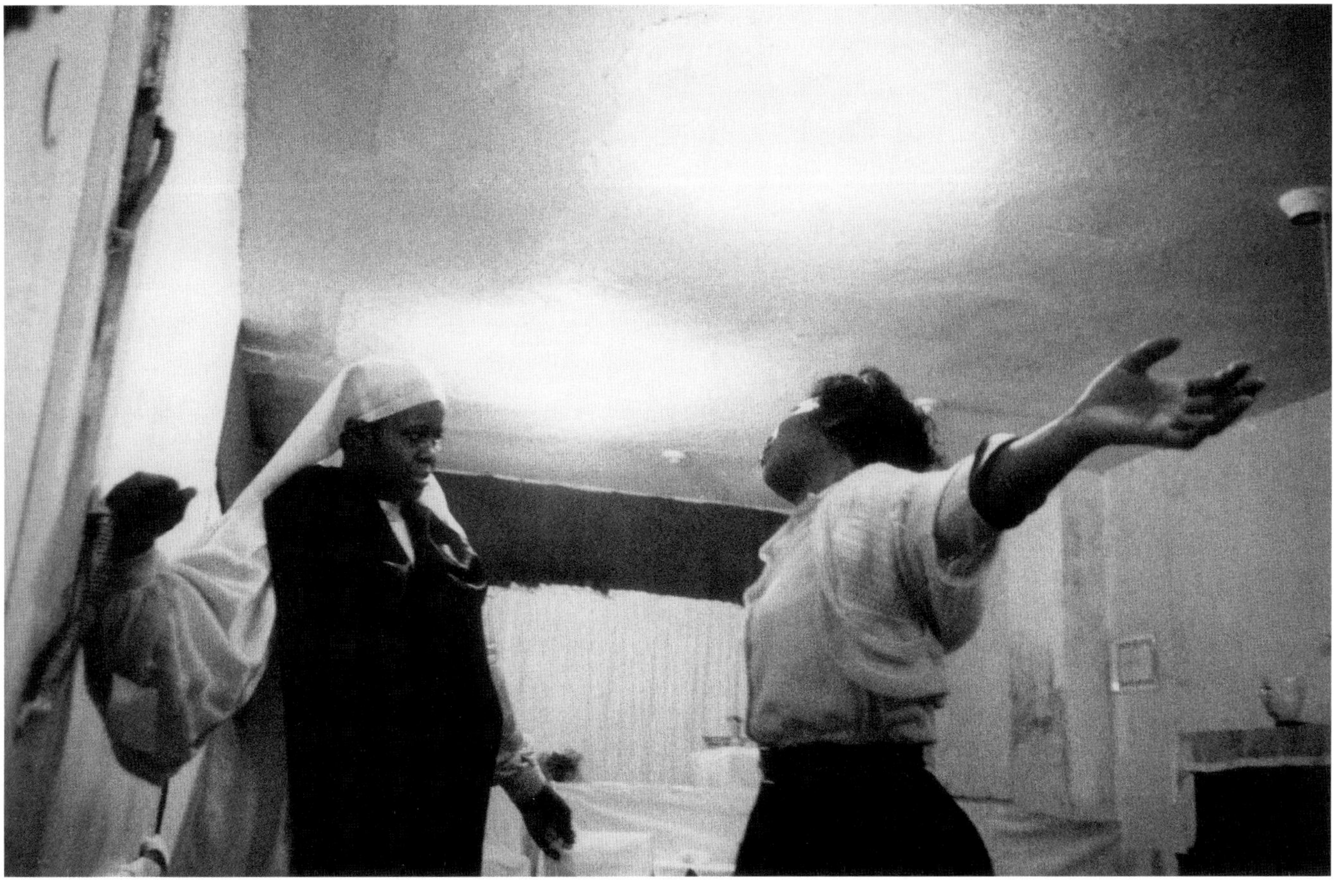

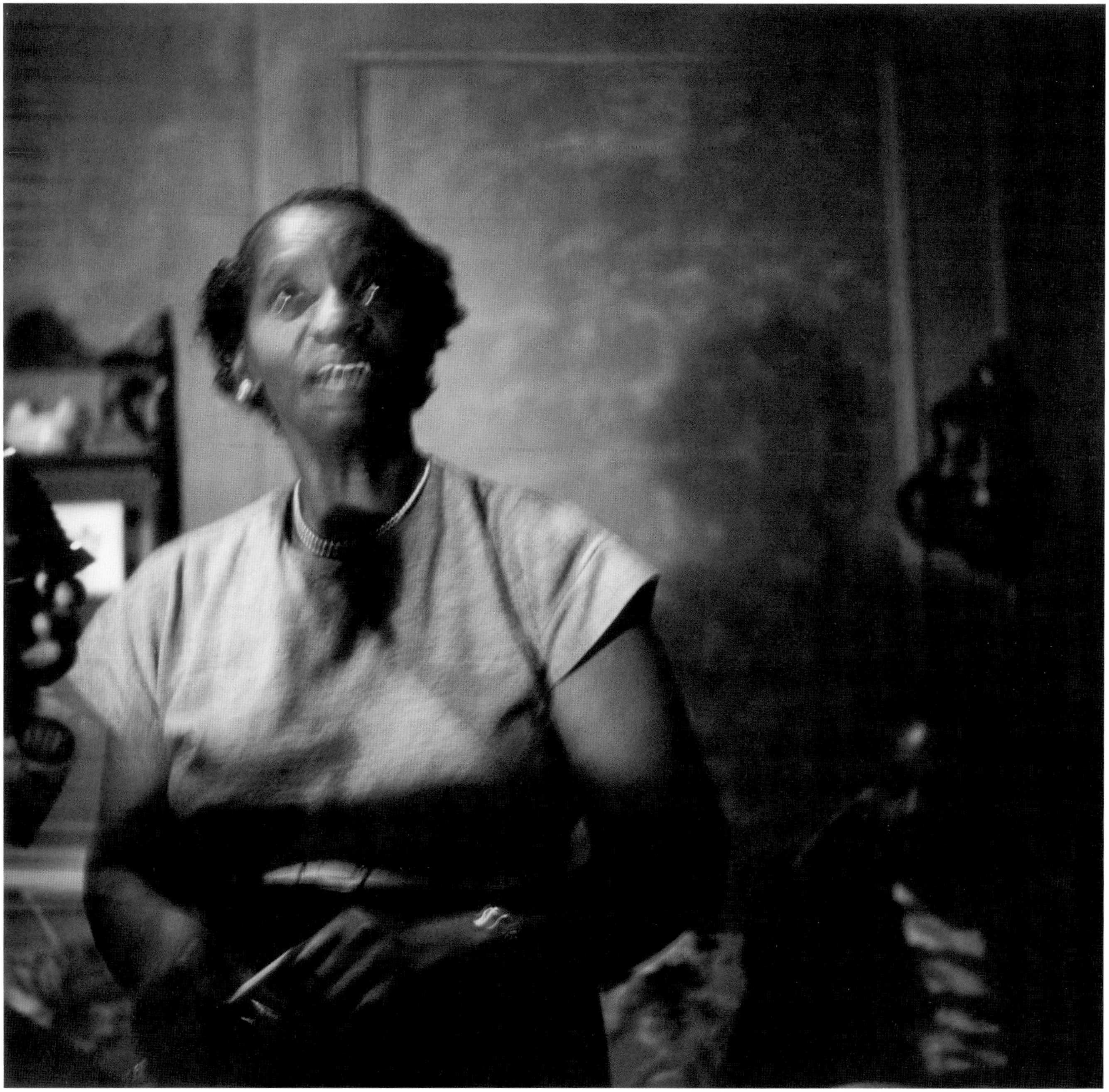

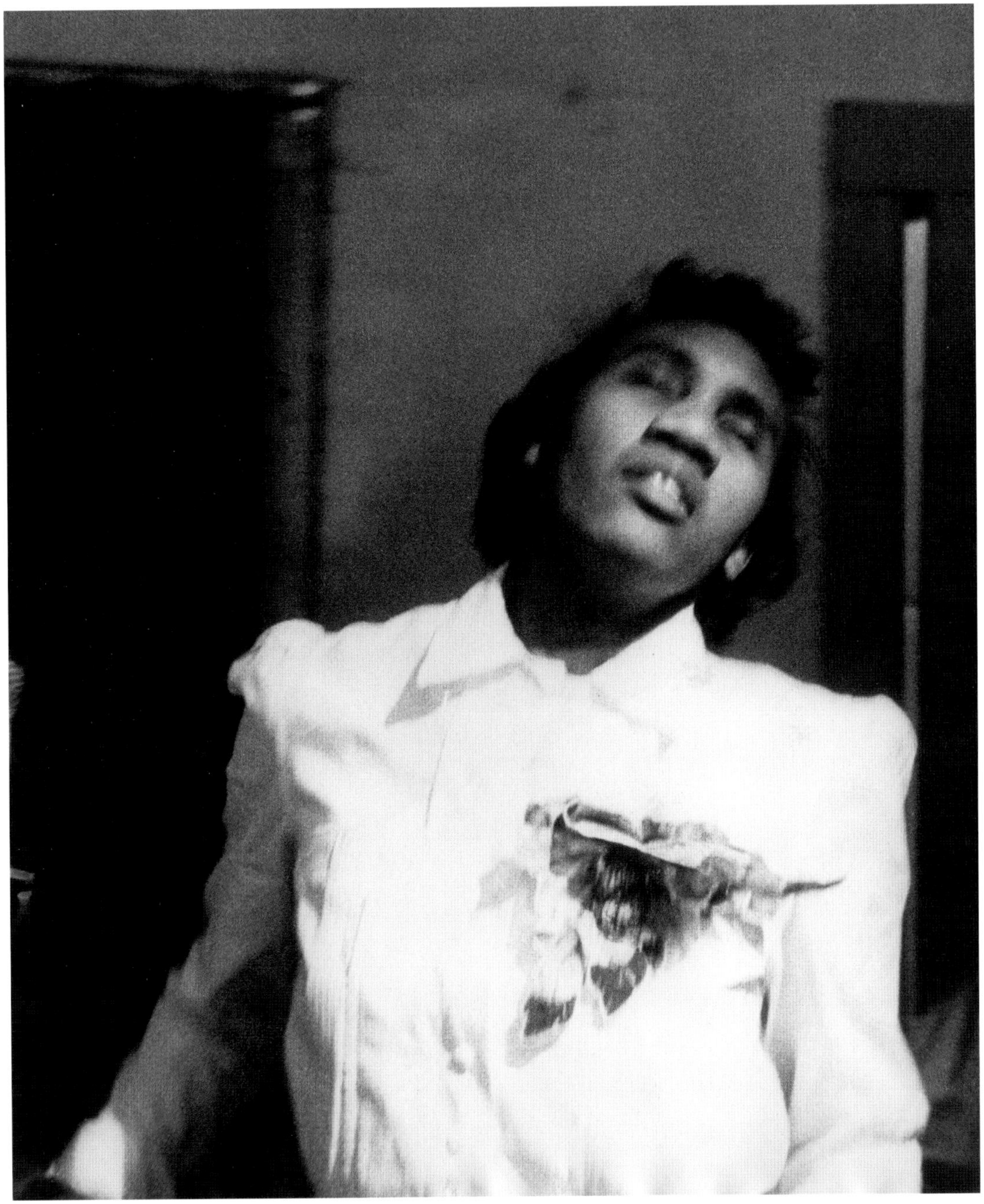

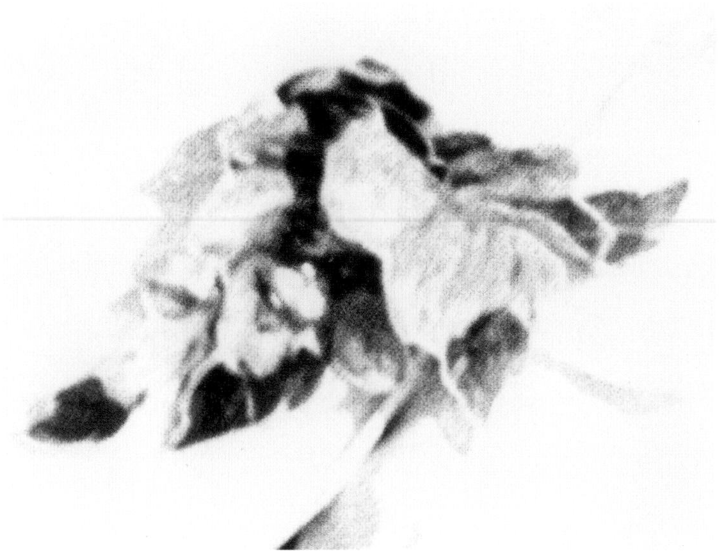

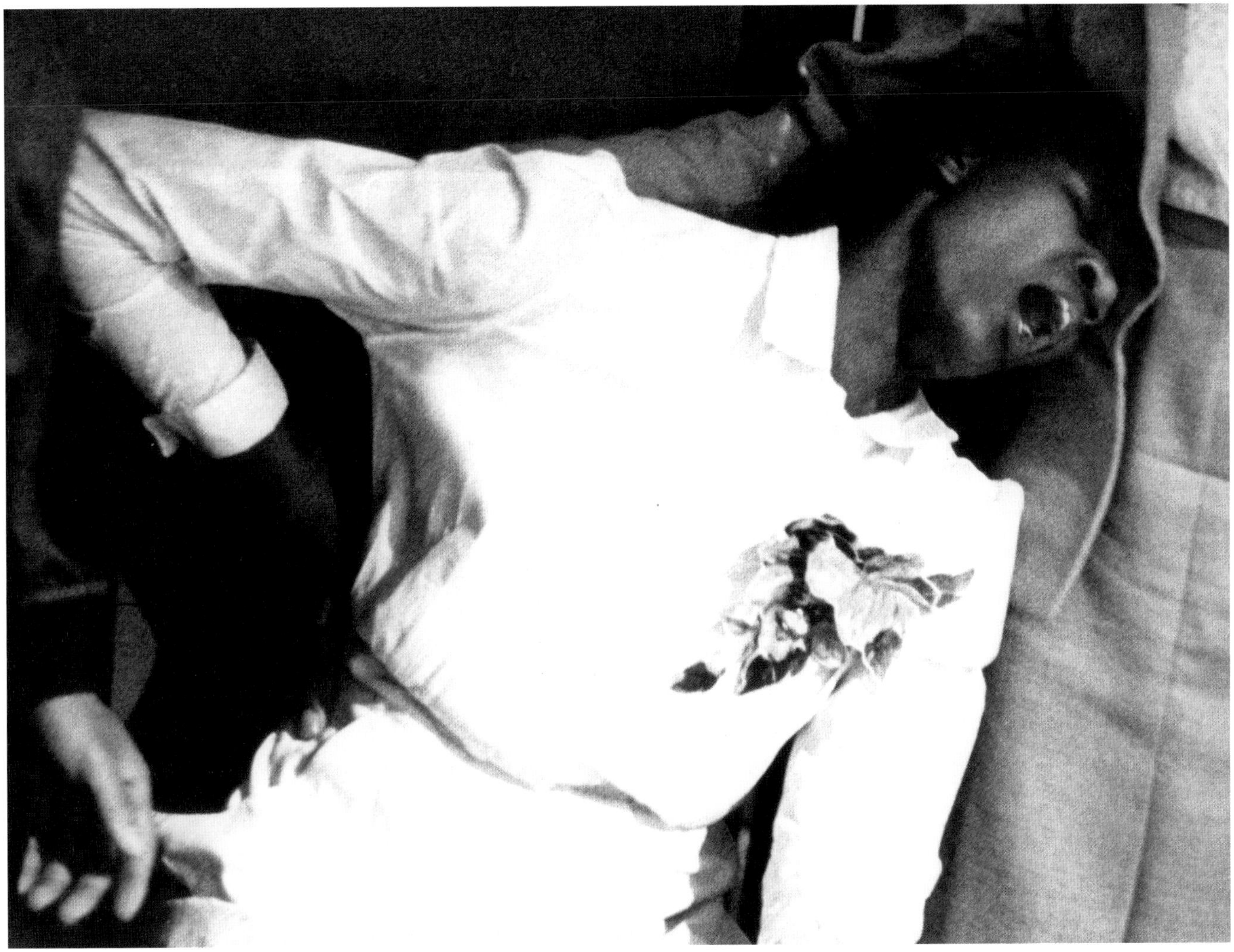

"I WANT MY CHILDREN TO KNOW JUST WHAT I KNOW."

Janie Hunter, Johns Island, South Carolina, 1964

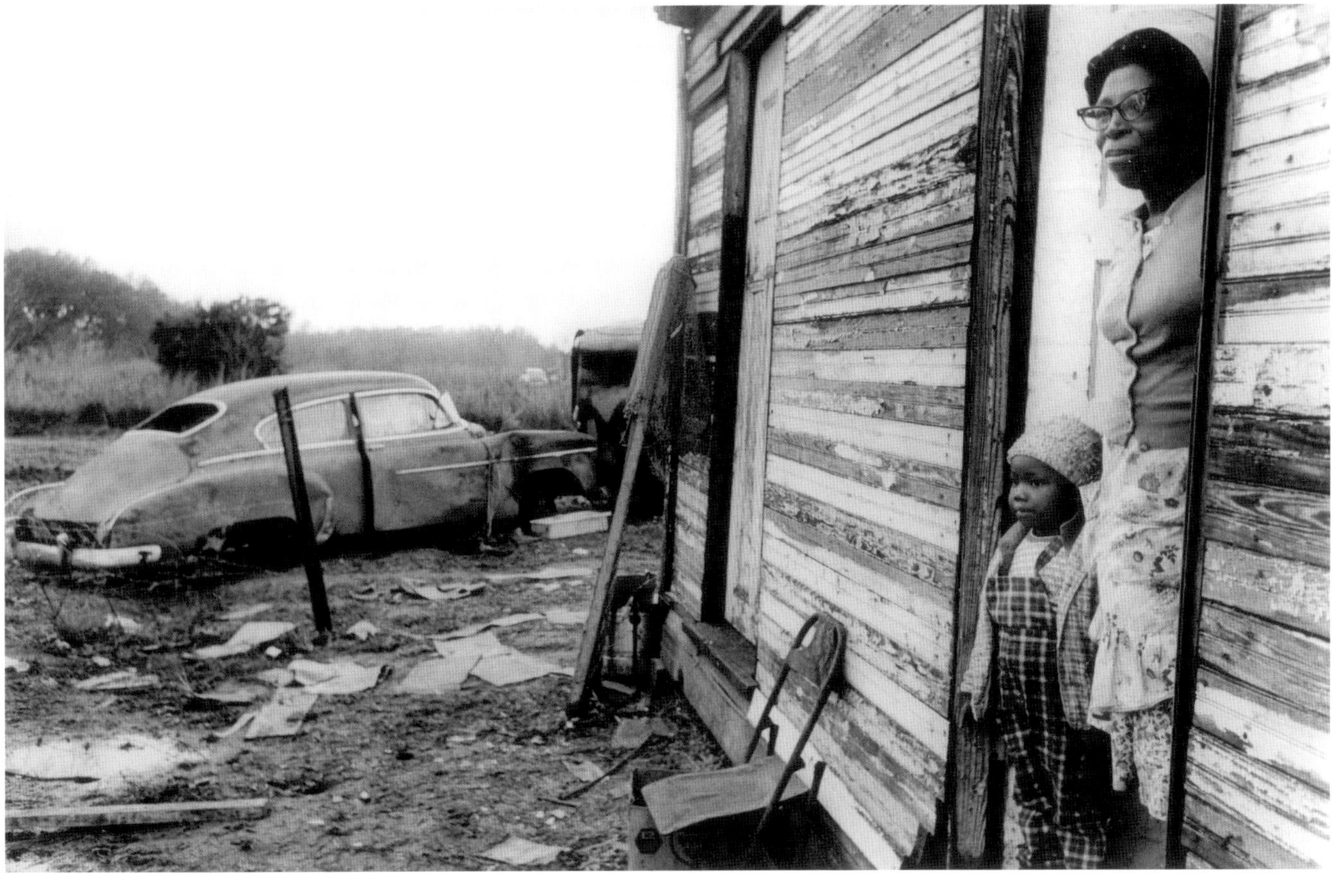

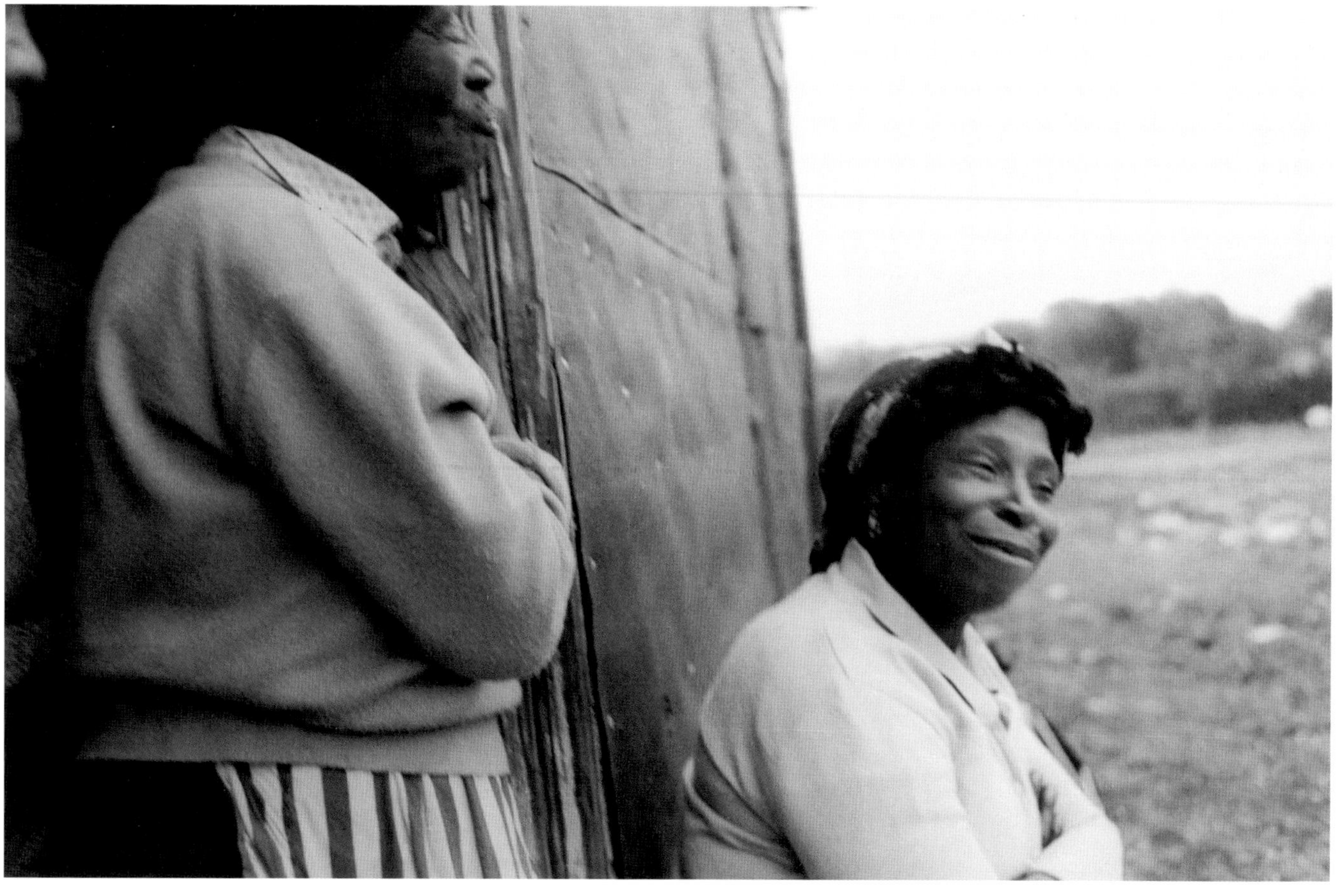

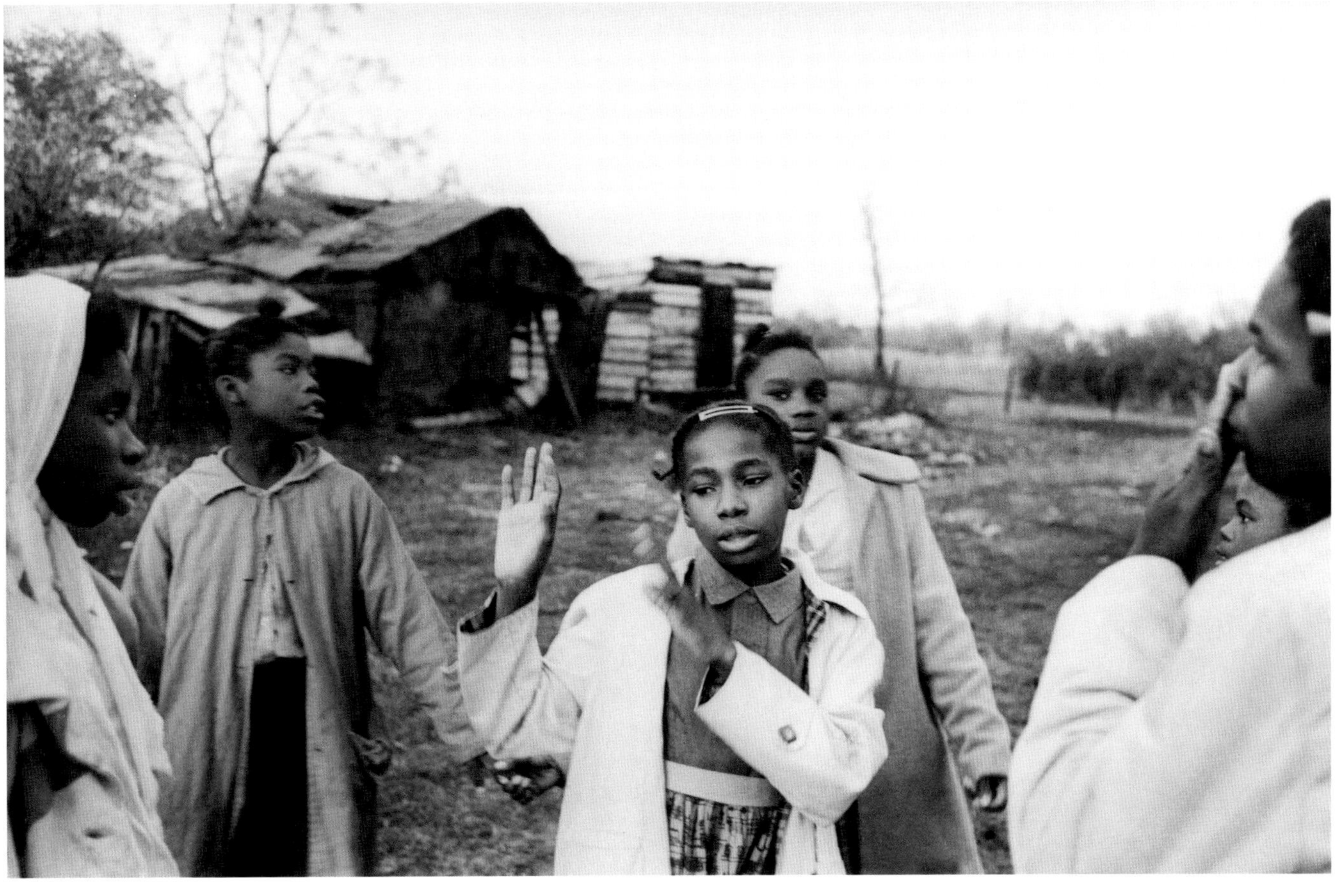

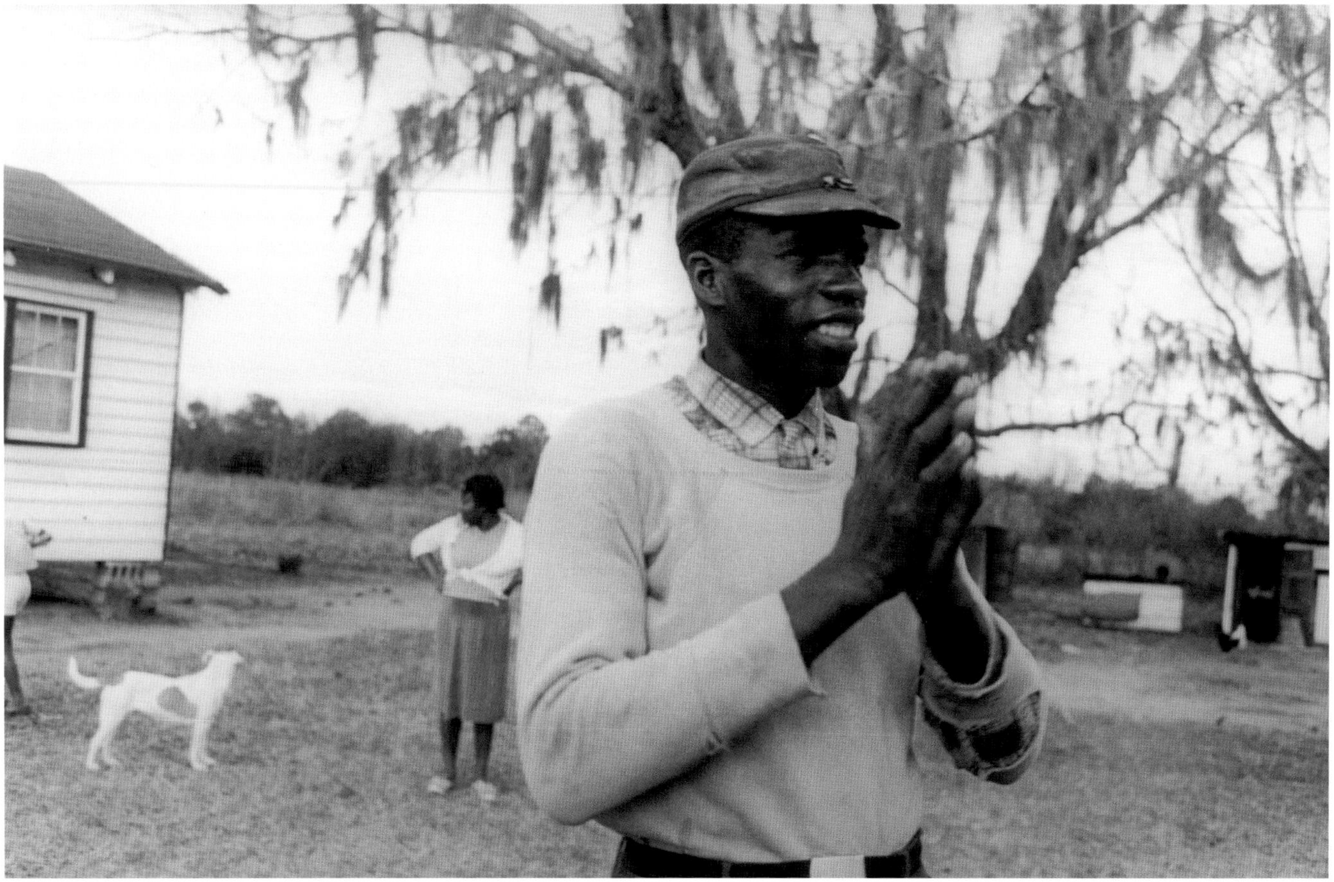

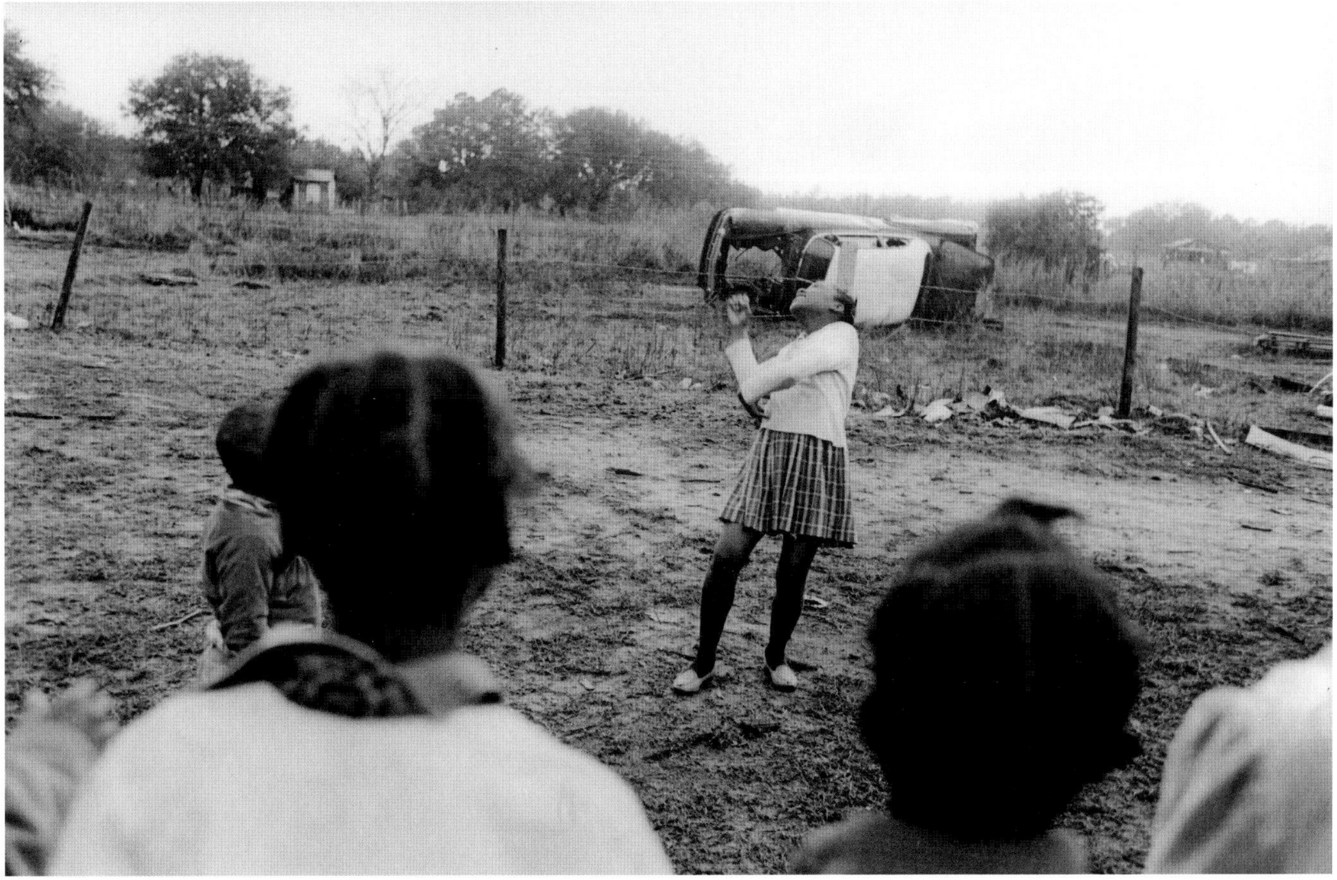

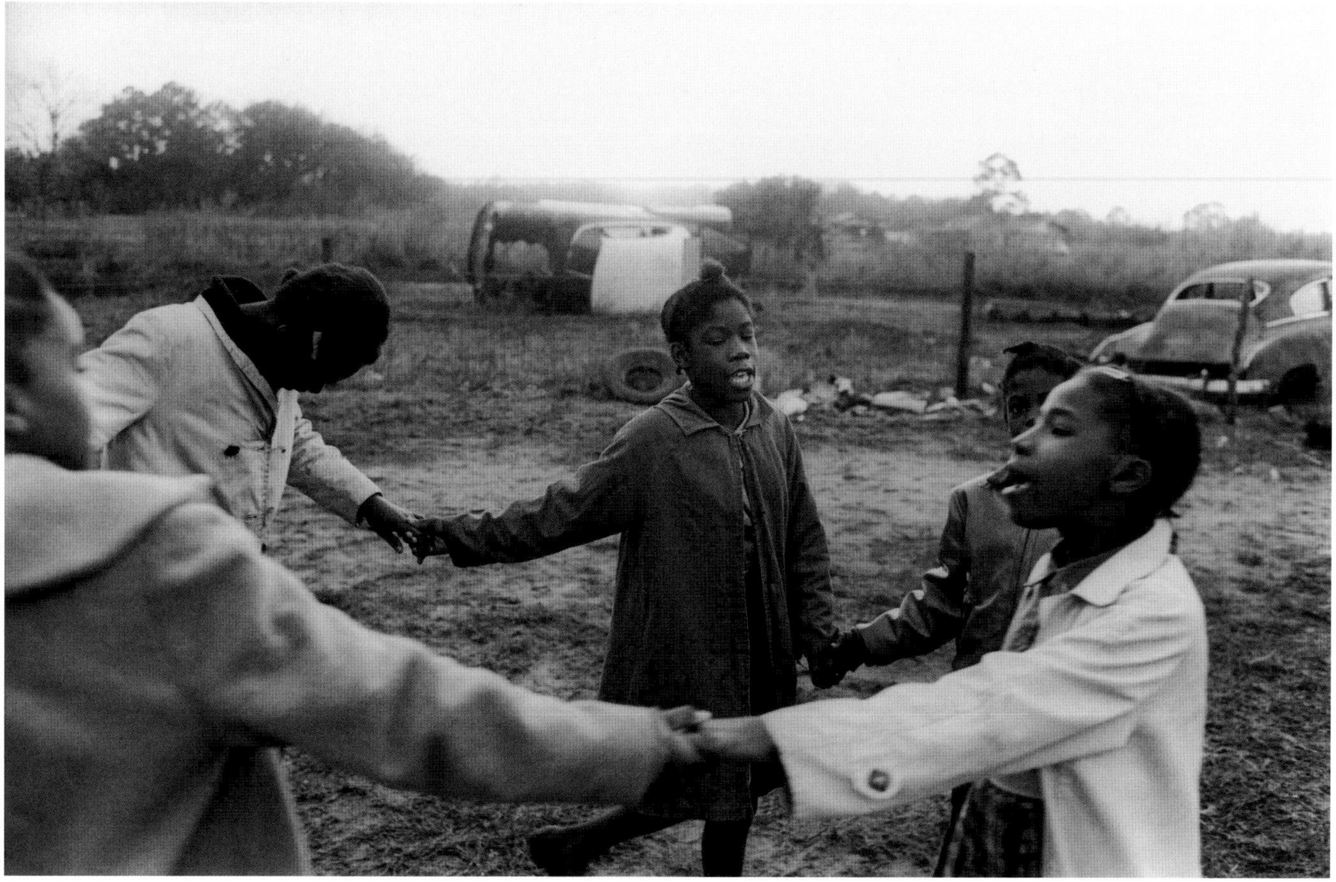

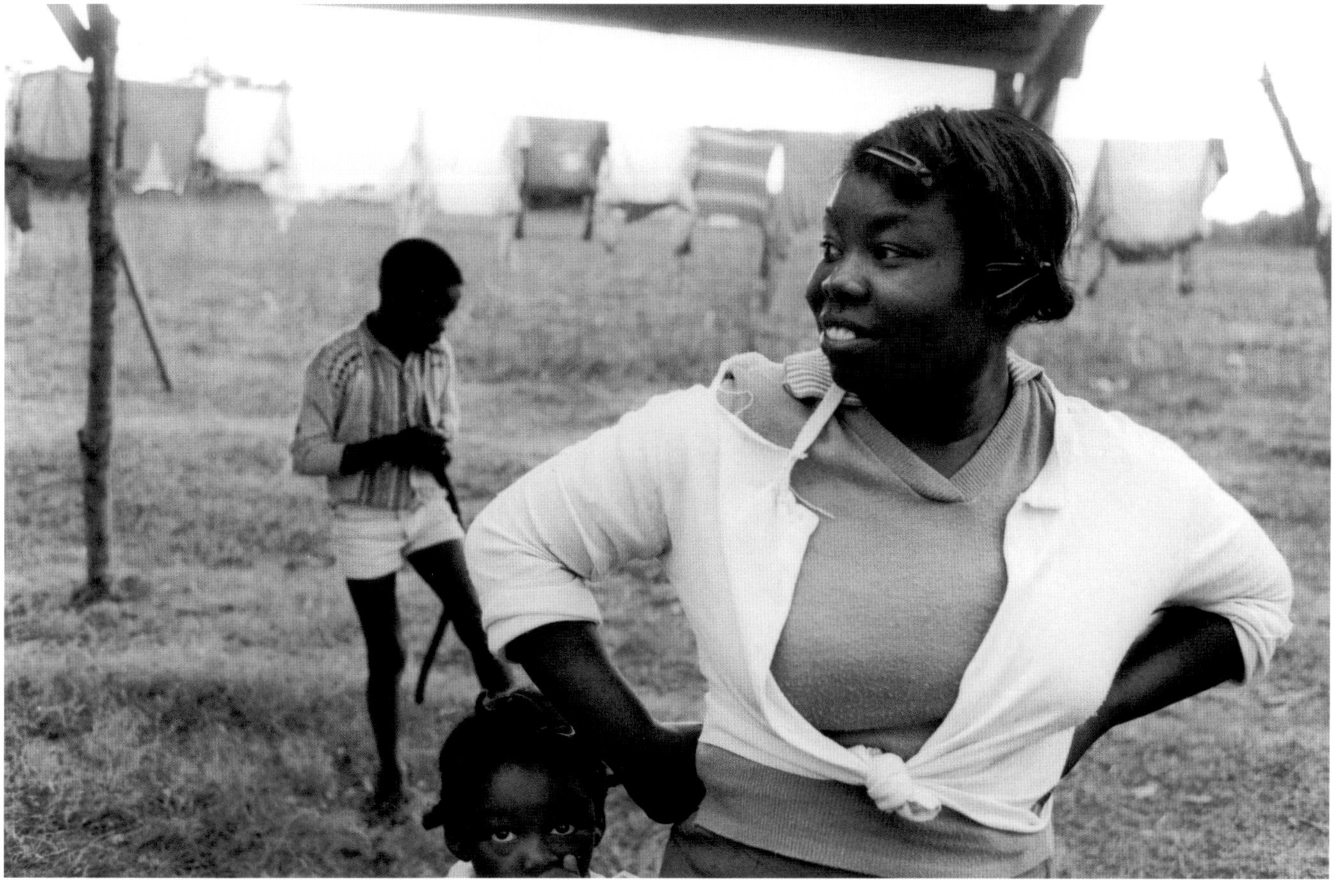

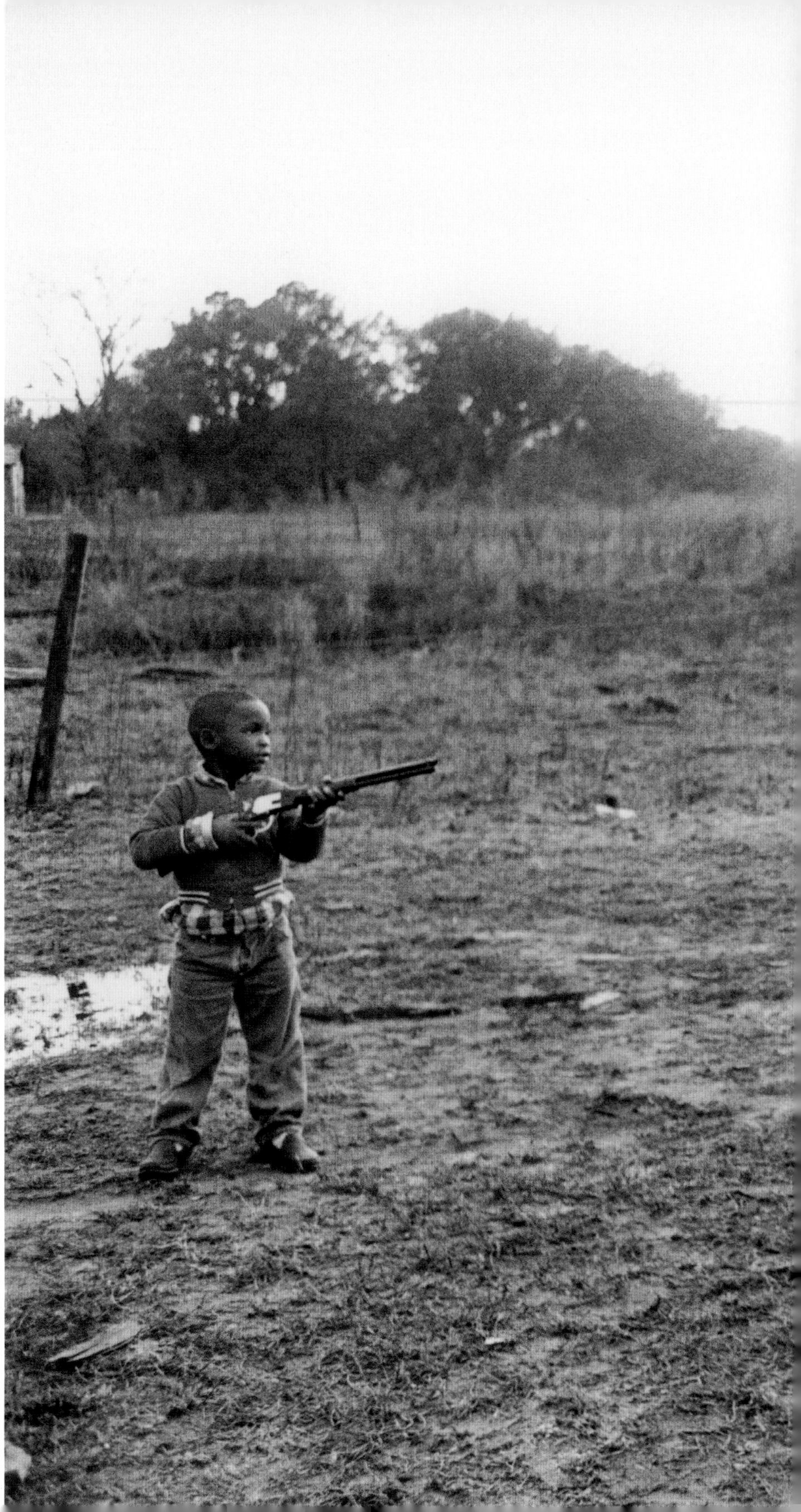

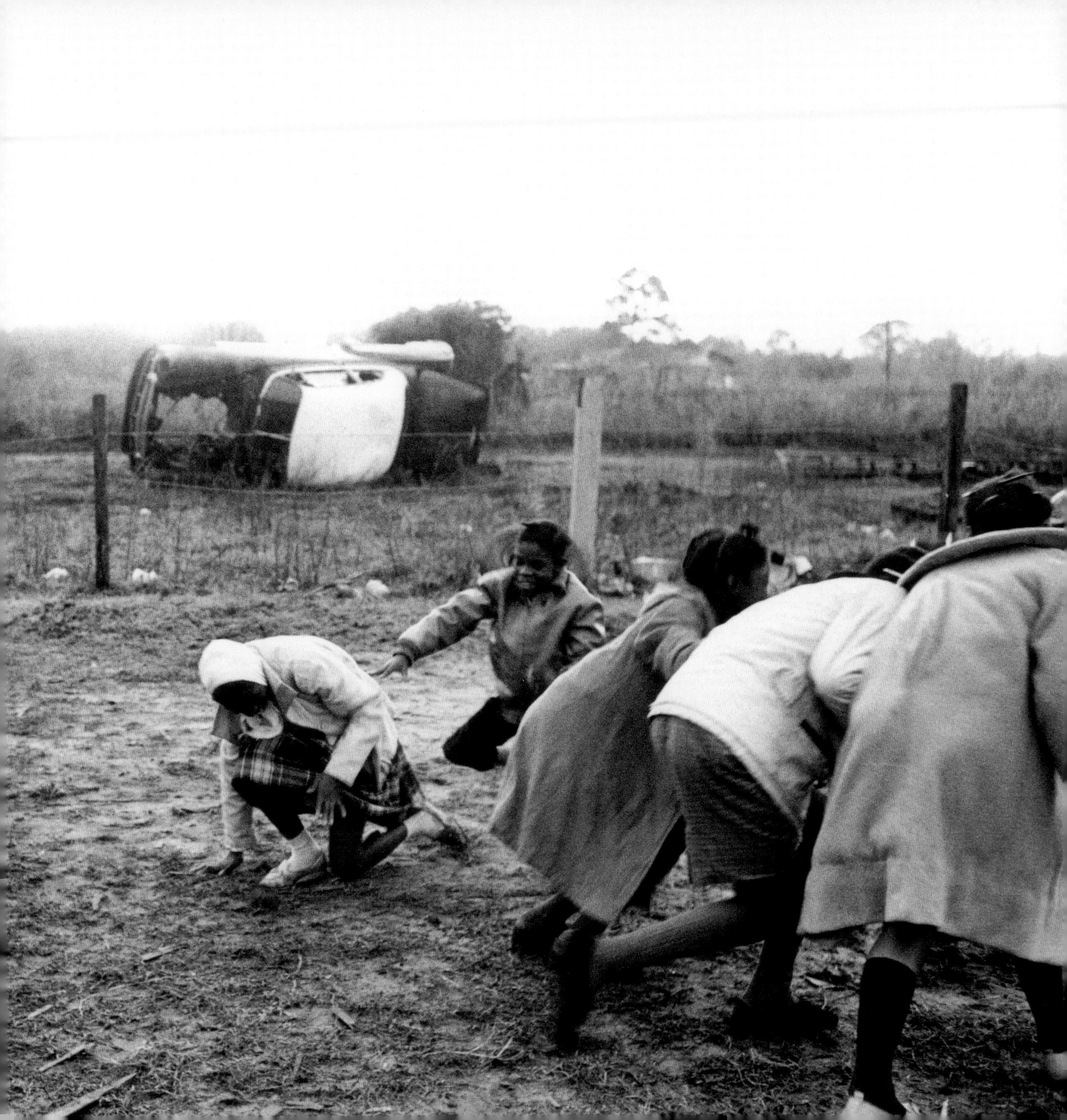

WALKING in THE LIGHT

"Walking in the Light" is a photographic journey towards the gospel music witnessed in the churches of East New York, and in New Haven street games, in the gospel shouts of blind Reverend Gary Davis, in the darkness of a boxing gym and the blackness of coal shovelers. In a small Harlem congregation, worshippers found spiritual release in trances and dances, while Gullah children in the Carolina Sea Islands connected to African ancestors through games.

Despite the nightmare of slavery and racial discrimination, African music has shaped the essential American sound in popular and religious music. It developed in dialog with European musical traditions, and infused them with a unique power.

The religious forms of black music in America have influenced everything from spirituals to gospel, soul music, and the vocal styles heard in popular music. Within African American communities, gospel music holds a powerful place. It remains as the central core to spiritual life, always performed with passion, style and depth ... and the conviction that there is a better life than this one.

In gospel churches where I photographed, the music making revealed inner sounds that can be seen on the face of the singer: soulful expressions, and the intensity of a prayer where raw feeling is laid bare, and the quality of light illuminates the face of a child ... The camera rendered all this in black-and-white images.

In 1955 Herbert Matter (1907–1984) invited me to make sound recordings in gospel churches for his film project in the black churches. He had been attracted to jazz as a young man in Switzerland. He talked of how this music had led him to Paris. Later in America he filmed jazz dancing at the

Savoy Ballroom in Harlem. He was seeking to find the sources of jazz dancing in the ecstatic dances that overtook people in religious trances. He listened to tape recordings I had made of the blind gospel singer Reverend Gary Davis, and invited me to assist him. I was with him at events in Harlem and East New York. These were some of my first forays into photography. They connected with film, music and dance.

I had heard "Negro" spirituals as a child, sung by my parents in a sincere and evocative way ... but I knew nothing of the life the music came from. My father had two books of "American Negro Spirituals" that he had acquired in 1925. They still sit on my shelves. "Negro" music was enjoyed and respected from a distance in my young life. The sound of gospel music and spirituals contained feelings and emotional jubilation that I never encountered anywhere else.

As I grew, this music led me away from home, and to a wider view of America.

At a summer camp the kitchen staff were all black folks from rural South Carolina. They would sing around the piano at night "Walk Around My Bedside Lord." Isaac Davis was a worker who cleaned the sewer pipes, played guitar and sang "Going to Kansas City." They all were housed in small cabins behind the barn. Separated and isolated from the campers, their places resembled slave quarters. This was my first encounter with authentic black home-based music.

TWO BLOCKS FROM YALE

Photography, art and music have been braided together in my life. At Yale Art School, the camera led me away from the studio and from middle-class life. Some of my first subjects as a photographer were about black musical experiences.

Photos of black kids in the streets of New Haven echo collages and paintings I was doing in my art school studio. The camera recorded my wanderings and the adventures it led to. I had come to art school as a painter, and left as a photographer. The photography program at Yale started by Herbert Matter gave me unexpected freedom to explore my own intuitions.

My basement apartment was just two blocks from Yale, by an old run-down neighborhood. Standing on Oak Street I photographed the games of black kids, noticing how they animated the street, and how the space was changed and affected by their placements. I imagined it as if it were a theatrical stage set or a contemporary dance recital.

With the Yale campus far behind, the improvised life in the street got to me. Gypsies beckoned me into their storefront, and led me to their family behind the curtains. I was given access to an exotic unknown world which was quite mundane (the kids were named Frankie and Perry after pop singers Frank Sinatra and Perry Como).

In the black neighborhood around 1954, I ventured into record stores and bought records by Blind Lemon Jefferson, Lightnin' Hopkins and a 78 by Blind Gary Davis, and heard rhythm and blues music coming from dance halls in the months before Elvis arrived on the scene. In fact, when I first heard his music broadcast from a block away, I thought it was Leadbelly. Sometimes I hopped on a New Haven city bus and traveled to the end of the line ... then walked back to town having adventures with the camera. Soot-covered track workers shoveled coal before immense piles of coal. The darkness of a boxing gym was welcoming and didn't evoke violence. The street life contrasted with the affluent and proper attitudes of Yale undergraduates. Somehow I wasn't interested in photographing on the Yale campus.

REVEREND GARY DAVIS

Blind Reverend Gary Davis had come to New York City in the 1940s, and lived off his music singing on street corners and in gospel churches. I was seventeen when I first heard him performing two pieces at the Leadbelly Memorial Concert. I couldn't believe how he got those sounds out of his guitar. A few years later I was asked to bring him to a hootenanny in the city, and went to pick him up from his home in Harlem. After that I visited him at home and lugged a heavy wire recorder to capture his music. His living space was small, and filled with family and little kids. Along with the brilliant guitar playing, his powerful singing and shouting in the room was overwhelming. Later, in 1953, I obtained a portable tape recorder to record him better. I photographed around his music and followed him into his neighborhood where he sang and played at a local grocery store. My parents and I were invited to a gospel show in Harlem where he was being honored. Not long after that he became a popular performer in the folk music revival, singing gospel, blues and ragtime to white audiences at clubs and concerts. He inspired many performers such as Dave Van Ronk, Jorma Kaukonen and Bob Dylan. He once said, "I'm here in your midst as a black man, like a fly in buttermilk. It ain't how a thing looks, though, it's what it is."

GOSPEL CHURCHES

After art school I continued with the gospel music project on my own in New York City. Longing for the energizing music of the churches, one Sunday I took the subway to Harlem and walked around listening for that sound. I heard it coming from a fifth floor window. In the building, following a dark hallway and five flights of stairs leading to a door where the sound came from, I knocked, and eventually someone let me into a room with people singing, clapping and dancing. Six of the seven people there were in a religious trance. I was told to come back in a few hours, so I waited, returned and spoke with the priestess who said it would be OK to return another time. In the following weeks, as I photographed in that room I was filled with their spirit, music, trance, dance and raw energy. It filled all my senses, and made me feel that there wasn't room for anything else.

In ways which couldn't be done now, I attempted to photograph the energy generated in that room. I felt that the church members had found release and transformation within the music, in reaction to the painful constrictions of New York City life. Going to Harlem alone to fill my own musical craving, I had witnessed a black community's spiritual release.

Around that time I read James Baldwin's book "Go Tell It on the Mountain" which describes the experience in the churches. His moving prose gave great insight into the religious services.

SEA ISLAND

In 1964 I had heard the singer Janie Hunter at a festival, and wanted to know more about the African-based dances her children and grandchildren were doing in her rural community on Johns Island, near Charleston, South Carolina. On the island, eight-year old kids performed African games, followed immediately by 1920s Charleston dance steps, Kung Fu moves and modern Motown choreography. Within moments they shifted gears from one era to another.

Janie Hunter was the driving force. She said, "I want my children to know just what I know." She sang, "In this slavery land, we're going to have a good time, way by and by." She listened to B.B. King, and told me, "I likes blues music and gospel: they've got feelings."

I visited a local dance hall on the island in 1975, the music was supplied by a disc jockey with two turntables and a drummer who provided rhythmic transitions as the records were changed. In this manner the music was continuous, the changes were seamless, and the dancing never stopped. For me, this was new, a forecast of disco music ... which became popular soon after.

In the traditional churches on the island, gospel singing and community organizing were happening together. This was the Civil Rights era and my friend Guy Carawan was helping assemble things there (see his book "Ain't You Got a Right to the Tree of Life?").

I was able to film the children's dances and some of Janie Hunter's songs, but a local black community organization wouldn't permit me to film in the dance halls. They said it wasn't for a white guy to represent their music. Despite my frustration, I agreed with their position although it meant the end of my exploration. I had gone as far as was politically possible, and it became the conclusion of my journey photographing black music in America.

ACKNOWLEDGMENTS

Thanks to Herbert Matter who, through his example and photography classes, allowed me to find what was already inside of me. He was truly a friend and mentor … without his generosity and consideration, I probably wouldn't have become a photographer.

Thanks to the music which has guided my art; to Reverend Davis and Janie Hunter, and the anonymous gospel church members who allowed me access to their soulful ceremonies.

Thanks to Philip Brookman for criticism and encouragement. He's got an eye for meaning.

Thanks to Sid Kaplan for better prints from old negatives.

Thanks to Gerhard Steidl for helping artists realize their projects and visions – as beautiful books.

Photographs made in
New Haven, Connecticut, 1954 and 1955
Harlem, New York City, 1954, 1955 and 1957
East New York, 1956
Johns Island, South Carolina, 1964

Credits
Excerpts from James Baldwin's "Go Tell It on the Mountain," 1953. Copyright renewed. Reprinted by arrangement with the James Baldwin Estate.
Guy & Candie Carawan, "Ain't You Got a Right to the Tree of Life," University of Georgia Press, 1989

John Cohen's photographs courtesy L. Parker Stephenson

Cover snapshot of Reverend Gary Davis by John Cohen, Harlem, New York City, 1953

Recordings
"There Is No Eye: Music for Photographs," Smithsonian Folkways SFW40091
"If I Had My Way: Early Home Recordings," Reverend Gary Davis, Smithsonian Folkways SFW40123
"Been in the Storm So Long," Smithsonian Folkways FW03842 / FS 3842

First edition published in 2015

 ///// Book design: John Cohen, Gerhard Steidl, Sarah Winter ///// Scans by Steidl ///// Separations by Steidl's digital darkroom ///// Production and printing: Steidl, Göttingen ///// Steidl, Düstere Str. 4, 37073 Göttingen, Germany, Phone +49 551 49 60 60, Fax +49 551 49 60 649 ///// mail@steidl.de ///// steidl.de ///// ISBN 978-3-86930-772-5 ///// Printed in Germany by Steidl